Leo Sayer

Leo Sayer is a clown who has turned serious performer. When he first made his bow on the showbiz scene, singing a song called "The Show Must Go On" – which topped the singles charts – he was wearing a clown's outfit and make-up.

But he did that, he now admits, purely to attract attention to himself. And who's going to deny that it worked?

Since then, though, the talented Sayer – who started out as a busker on the streets of London – has really made his mark. He has firmly established himself as an artist who can never be ignored for too long.

His first album, "Silverbird", was a best-seller. But after he took off his clown's costume and started playing it straight, Leo found even greater success. His second album, "Just a Boy", went gold, and his next single "Long Tall Glasses", smashed in the charts both in Britain and America.

More record hits followed fairly rapidly. Records like "Moonlighting", and the smash-hit "You Make Me Feel Like Dancing".

But it was in America, where he realised he was blossoming slowly in the world's toughest record field, that Leo was determined to make his mark. His first album produced in the States, "Endless Flight", took more than six months to make. And his manager Adam Faith insisted on getting some of America's top musicians to back Leo on the disc.

Leo Sayer is a young man who still refuses to be pigeon-holed. But he is tremendously ambitious. And he says quite candidly: "My aims are two-fold. One is to be as big as Elton John or that kind of artist. The other is longevity. I hope to be around for a very long time."

Tina Charles

TINA CHARLES is the most exciting and certainly the most delightful British singer to emerge as a truly international artist over the last year or so.

In 1976 alone, she sold more than four-and-a-half million records. This was the year when she really came through to become the most successful girl singer on the British pop scene.

Her records "I Love To Love", "You Set My Heart On Fire" and "Dance Little Lady" proved that she had more than her fair share of talent. Within only a few weeks of release, all three songs hit the charts in over a dozen countries, with "I Love to Love" scoring a gold in Britain.

She's only 23, but she has the voice and the musical control of a woman much older.

Yet this is not so surprising, really, for little Tina – a born-and-bred cockney from Bow, East London – has packed a lot of experience into those few years since she left school.

She actually cut her first disc, "Good To Be Alive", when she was only 15 . . . with Elton John playing piano on the record!

Tina then served her musical apprenticeship touring air bases and doing other gigs with a dance band. Slowly, she moved up the showbiz ladder to better-paid jobs, and toured with such stars as Tom Jones, Engelbert Humperdinck and Gilbert O'Sullivan. From there, she went into recording session work, vocally backing artists like Salena Jones and Steve Harley's Cockney Rebel.

Her first big hit record "I Love To Love" was the result of five years of hard work, she says. "But I'm grateful for all that. Looking back it was all very good experience for me."

Tina has now had hit records in countries all over the world – including Greece, Jamaica, Holland, Scandinavia, France, Belgium, South Africa, and Israel.

And as far as "Top of the Pops" is concerned, Tina has added a much needed bit of glamour to the show, as well as carrying the flag for female equality in the pop stakes.

TOP OF THE POPS ANNUAL 1978

Edited by Ken Irwin

SMOKIE, spelling out their name on the Top of the Pops set, during the show.

10 CC

Many honest-to-goodness rock fans must have been dreadfully disappointed when 10 cc, one of the best and hardest-working bands in the country, split up just over a year ago.

But they would undoubtedly have been far more sad if two of the four – Graham Gouldman and Eric Stewart – had not decided to carry on as a duo, with the name of 10 cc.

Originally formed in Manchester in 1972, 10 cc quickly proved themselves to be one of the most talented groups around on the rock scene.

Together, they churned out some rather super hit singles, including "Donna", "Rubber Bullets", "The Dean And I", and "I'm Not In Love".

But after the break-up of the group, Graham Gouldman and Eric Stewart immediately set out to prove all over again that they were still very much a vocal force to be reckoned with – and produced the bit hit number "The Things We Do For Love", as their first single together.

Since then, they've stayed remarkably in tune and are still rated among the best.

CONTENTS

We would like to thank all Record Companies and Publicists for kind permission to reproduce some of the photographs in this book.
Special thanks also go to Brian Clifford of the BBC, and the producers of Top of the Pops for their co-operation.

We thank:

A & M Records
Arista Records
Asylum Records
BBC
Tony Barrow International
Bell Records
Tony Brainsby
CBS Records
Chrysalis Records
Clifford Elson Publicity
EMI
Island Records
Magnet Records
MGM
Phonogram Records
Polydor Records
Rocket Records
RSO Records

Published in Great Britain by
World Distributors (Manchester) Limited.
A Member of the Pentos Group.
P.O. Box 111, 12 Lever Street, Manchester M60 1TS,
by arrangement with the British Broadcasting Corporation.

Designed by Artes Graphicae,
26 Harrison Street, London WE1H 8JE.

Printed in Great Britain by
Jarrold & Sons Limited, Norwich.

SBN 7235 0432 6

Status Quo

A lot has happened to Status Quo during their 14 years together. They've outgrown, and out-played most of their contemporaries. And there are very few groups around who have stuck together so faithfully for such a long time.

After a couple of record hits – when they were far too young to handle such success – they spent a long time in the wilderness, sorting themselves out and desperately trying to find a new sound.

They came back on the scene four or five years ago, quite obviously with more appeal as a curious mixture of rock and pop boogie band.

Since then, the jean-clad foursome have amassed a huge army of enthusiastic supporters, who happily help to make every concert they stage a "sell out".

They have emerged as one of Britain's hardest-working concert bands, and have scored with an impressive list of singles and albums in the record field. Their "Piledriver" LP put them back firmly in the charts, and they followed up with massive sellers in "Hello", "Quo", "On The Level" and "Blue For You".

With such vast experience behind them, the lads from Status Quo (Francis Rossi, Alan Lancaster, Rick Parfitt, and John Coughlan) are going to be around for a long time yet, you can be sure of that.

INTRODUCTION

Welcome to another edition of the top annual in TV pop music. Our fifth, in fact.

"Top of the Pops" is still the No. 1 pop show on television, in spite of all the competition from other programmes which are still trying to catch up on our success.

The programme is now in its 15th record-breaking year. . . . The longest-running TV pop show in the world.

This is the show on which all the top pop stars want to appear. But why does it remain so successful, year in and year out, with audiences, both young and old?

"Because the show reflects the very best in popular music – all kinds of pop music," says disc-jockey Jimmy Savile, one of the original deejays who is still with the programme after 14-plus years.

"It's one show I will never give up," says Jimmy. "No matter how many other TV shows I do – like 'Jim'll Fix It' – or how many radio programmes I work on, I will never want to stop doing 'Top of the Pops', because I still regard this programme as the corner-stone of my career.

"What's more, it's fun. And I like having fun in life, folks."

That, probably, is the reason for the show's never-ending success. Because it's FUN!

We hope you will keep on having fun, too, watching "Top of the Pops" during 1978. Because, when it comes to pop music, this is where it's all really at. Happy pop-viewing for another year!

5000 VOLTS

One group who have shot to the top in the last year is 5000 Volts. Some of their performances on "Top of the Pops" have been truly electrifying!

After their mammoth worldwide sales in 1975 with their very first record, "I'm On Fire", and then another monster hit with "Dr. Kiss Kiss", they firmly established themselves as one of the most inventive and dynamic groups around.

They came together almost by accident. Songwriter and vocalist Tony Eyers was looking for a group to help him record a new song, "I'm On Fire". He brought together three other session singers, and they added Tina Charles' voice to the disc. The result, a few months later, was a top-three hit record.

On the strength of this, they decided to stick together and form a regular working band. A second record, "Bye Love", was released early in 1976, but this only managed to get into the bottom of the charts.

Then, because of contractual problems, Tina Charles was replaced by singer Lynda Kelly. And suddenly – hey presto! 5000 Volts had hit on a completely new sound!

Lynda has been singing professionally since she was a teenager. Her husband Chris, who used to sing with the old Ivy League group, then took over as manager of 5000 Volts from Tony Eyers.

Apart from Lynda, the rest of the line-up is: Martin Jay and Martin Cohen, guitarists, keyboard player Mike Nelson, and drummer Kevin Wells.

Slik

Scotland has been producing more than its fair share of bands and pop artists over the last decade. Among those who have already found international success from North o' the Border are the Average White Band, Bay City Rollers, Alex Harvey, and Billy Connolly.

And SLIK are following hard on the heels of them all, determined to establish a niche for themselves.

They're another group who first appeared on "Top of the Pops" – early in 1976 – and have not looked back since.

They were originally called Salvation, but changed their name to Slik three years ago. Their clean-cut image is based on the original American college-boy look of the 1950s, and this has gone over in a big way, particularly with their hoards of Scottish fans.

THE G BAND

The G-BAND is unique, in that they started out purely as a musical backing group for the effervescent Gary Glitter . . . and outgrew the great Gary to reach for stardom on their own. And this they have very definitely achieved over the last few years.

The five-man outfit was happy to bask in the glory – albeit, the glory of the shadows – of Gary Glitter when he emerged as a world-wide "heart-throb" of the teenyboppers.

But it soon became abundantly clear to all around them that the Glitter Band were too good to stay in the background for an indefinite period. So they began to make records on their own, while still backing Gary on concert tours and on records. In fact, they helped Gary achieve global sales of more than 17 million records.

It wasn't long before the Glitter boys hit the Top 20 with a string of best-selling songs of their own – "Angel Face", "Just For You", "Let's Get Together Again", "Goodbye My Love", "Tears I Cried", "Love In The Sun", "People Like You".

They broke loose from Gary in 1974, and soon after their record "People Like You" hit the Top Five in the charts, they shortened their name to the G-Band, and later signed a long-term world-wide recording contract with CBS Records.

The G-Band write most of their own songs. Their first album for CBS was "Paris Match", and was produced in Paris by Mike Leander. The boys themselves wrote nine of the ten tracks on the album.

Guys 'n' Dolls

When GUYS 'N' DOLLS first came together as a vocal group, late in 1974, they soft-pedalled it on publicity – particularly where Julie Forsyth was concerned.

For blonde-haired Julie was the long-legged and attractive daughter of Bruce Forsyth, and it was felt that this was bound to lead to more personal publicity for Julie than the rest of the group.

Julie was only 16 at the time, but she handled the whole situation remarkably well – like a showbiz veteran, in fact.

The whole group – and their handlers – were determined that the image of the group was the all-important thing, and not any individual member of it.

Guys 'n' Dolls were carefully handpicked from an audition involving more than 300 singers. The Guys chosen were Dominic Grant, David Van Day and Paul Griggs. And the Dolls were Martine Howard, Thereze Bazar, and Julie Forsyth.

Once the group was formed, a massive publicity machine moved in on their behalf. And within two months, the Guys 'n' Dolls had their first record, "There's A Whole Lot Of Loving", released – and it shot to No. 2 in the charts and earned them a silver disc.

They immediately built themselves a teenybop following, with a lot of their fans, they say, coming from the six-to-sixteen age bracket.

With TV shows, "live" concerts, a spell in variety at the London Palladium and a tour with comedian Freddie Starr, by the end of 1976 Guys 'n' Dolls had firmly established themselves as Britain's new No. 1 clean-cut glamour group.

Their follow-up records, "Here I Go Again", "Let's All Get Together" and "You Don't Have To Say You Love Me", rocketed them into the charts again . . . and again.

They've now had hit records, too, in countries as diverse as Holland, Germany, Japan, South Africa, Spain, and Australia.

Kursaal Flyers

If anyone is really seeking evidence that the road to the top in the pop field is a long, hard haul . . . then they need look no further than the Kursaal Flyers.

Over the last year, the Kursaal Flyers, the rock and rhythm group who hail from Southend, have literally forced their way to the top through sheer guts and determination.

A few years ago, they were being "written off" as just another clumsy run-of-the-mill musical outfit who didn't know where they were going.

They were even featured in a BBC TV programme, spotlighting the heartache and the pain of a pop group who couldn't make the grade. Strangely enough, this proved to be something of a turning point for the lads from Southend. For it was after the TV show

that their luck changed, and their fortunes took a distinct upward rise.

They originated, in 1973, as a six-man group. There was Paul Shuttleworth, as vocalist, Vic Collins (pedal steel, bass, guitar), Graeme Douglas (guitar, and vocals), Richie Bull (banjo, bass, guitar), Will Birch (drums), and Dave Hatfield (bass). And they started off performing a strange mixture of virtually everything . . . country-and-western, soul and rock 'n' roll.

Most of them had played with various small-time bands around Southend, but Richie Bull was a highly talented banjo player who has already worked on several LP records. Richie was the only full professional among them.

It was at the end of 1974, after they'd started to branch out and get the occasional music gigs in London, that they decided – with the exception of one, Dave Hatfield – to turn professional.

But it then took two years of hard slogging before they were signed up on a recording contract by Jonathan King's U.K. label, and made two LPs, "Chocs Away" and "The Great Artiste".

Then came a change in record companies – the Flyers flew off to CBS Records, and took on Mike Batt, notable hit-maker, as their new record producer.

They finally hit the Big Time late in 1976 by breaking into the charts. And this is a habit they intend to try and continue.

Sailor

Sailor – a clean-cut and remarkably likeable group of blokes – had to shake off a considerable amount of criticism when they were first launched, back in 1974.

For a start, some of the more serious music papers accused them of sounding too much like Roxy Music. Then they were given the tag of appealing only to the "intellectual" band of pop followers . . . the debby daughters, and teenage lads who drove Daddy's Rover when their own sports cars were up for service!

Their appearance didn't help, for they dressed up rather self-consciously in white sailor-suits.

They shot to the top in 1975 with their smash-hit single "Glass of Champagne" – accompanied by various appearances on "Top of the Pops" which undoubtedly helped to establish them. They followed up in 1976 with the biggie "Girls, Girls, Girls", and then "Stiletto Heel".

Georg Kajanus, who writes most of their songs and plays twelve-string guitar, says: "When I was accused by some critics of copying Roxy Music's style for 'Glass of Champagne', it wasn't fair. I was really using what I felt was a particular English sound which was prevalent on the scene to get us the hit and the attention. You won't find another track on any of our albums which is similar. And there is nothing anywhere else to compare with the sound of our nickelodeon."

The giant nickelodeon is really Sailor's biggest musical gimmick. This is played jointly by Henry Marsh and Phil Pickett.

The fourth member of the group is Grant Serpell, the drummer. He says: "The strange thing about Sailor is that we all come from very different musical backgrounds. Georg tends to like folk oriented music, Phil likes soul, Henry goes for rock. And I'm a jazz man.

"We all decided the one ingredient missing in most pop music today seemed to be charm – and that is the ingredient we hope has added to our style."

STEVE HARLEY

COCKNEY REBEL

You could call him The Muhammad Ali of the Pop World. Steve Harley is the name . . . and he has never exactly been a shy one.

Over the past few years, Harley, the lad from New Cross, South East London, has rather enjoyed "blowing his own trumpet".

When he was on the way up, with his group Cockney Rebel, he amused the music paper journalists – and infuriated others – by boldly announcing that he was a musical genius, and it was only a matter of time before he became a Superstar.

Then, once he'd "arrived", he decided that the only way to stay on top was to keep telling people just how good he really was.

Miraculously, it worked. Harley found what he was looking for . . . a string of hit records sent him rocketing to the top in this country. And at the end of 1975 Cockney Rebel embarked on their first major tour of America – and "sold" themselves completely.

Harley is certainly the most outspoken and controversial star to hit the pop scene in a long time.

He first came to our notice back in 1973. Steve had already "served his time" as a folk singer, and he got together a band which he called Cockney Rebel, and quickly landed a recording contract with EMI.

Originally trained as a local paper journalist, Harley knew all the tricks of the trade, and when it came to giving Press interviews he thoroughly enjoyed himself.

In fact, it took him less than three years to prove his point about becoming a superstar.

But having found success with Cockney Rebel, Harley, for purely personal reasons, broke up the band – and four months later, when the critics were saying he was finished, he got together a completely new band under the same name.

With the album "Timeless Flight", Harley really emphasised that he was a very special musical talent. This was doubly confirmed with his next album, "Love's A Prima Donna".

"Cockney Rebel are not just something I look upon as my backing group," says Steve. "We are all in the business together, and I'm proud to be part of such a group."

It's not his image he worries about, he says – but the music he produces. "When all the pioneers have pioneered, the martyrs have been martyred, the latest American hypes hyped, it all boils down to just the music," he says philosophically.

Few rock bands can look back over the past year or so with as much satisfaction as Thin Lizzy.

The four lads who make up the group (lead singer and bass guitarist Phil Lynott, Scott Gorham and Brian Robertson on lead guitars, and Brian Downey on drums) have been struggling so hard together for so many years that, at times, it must have seemed like they would never quite make the grade.

Now, all that has changed. Their hard work has miraculously turned into satisfying success.

It really all happened for them in 1976. Within the space of six months the band jumped from near the bottom of the first division to the top.

They were voted by readers of "Melody Maker" as "The Brightest Hope of 1976" – and they have since certainly fulfilled that confidence.

They finally broke through as a top rock outfit by getting into the charts with the scintillating "The Boys Are Back In Town", which like the album it was taken from, "Jailbreak", was a Top Ten hit and a big seller throughout the world.

Then they released another album, "Johnny The Fox", which was so good it really confirmed the Thin Lizzy boys were here to stay.

In America, too, they really made their mark. The records "Jailbreak" and "The Boys Are Back In Town" put them high in the US album and single charts, and on only their second tour of the States they were warmly and enthusiastically acclaimed as one of the best British bands to cross the Atlantic.

There, they received outstanding critical praise in the Press. Such as . . . "Thin Lizzy offers a compelling blend of professionalism and aggression" – Rolling Stone magazine.

"This band has got it all" – Chicago Sun Times.

"Thin Lizzy immediately established their authority with the sell-out crowd and never let up" – Los Angeles Times.

Such reviews were a fitting compliment to a band who had really served their apprenticeship . . . and are now working hard at staying at the top of the tree.

ELECTRIC LIGHT ORCHESTRA

"They're different!" ... That's the phrase which has become synonymous with the group Electric Light Orchestra. And all the lads in the group take it as a compliment. For that's exactly what they set out to be . . . original!

Jeff Lynne, who has led the group since 1972, objects to the term "classical rock" that has so frequently been applied to ELO – because of their intermittent inclusion of snippets by Beethoven and Greig in both their live stage shows and on the occasional record album.

But this "classical" tag is not really so surprising, because the string section of ELO were all formerly in English symphony orchestras.

Yet Jeff Lynne insists: "The string section have all been classically trained. But I know only a few classical pieces, myself. And my favourite group, and greatest influence, was always the Beatles. I think our music borders on a lot of different styles."

Orginally formed by that bearded Birmingham musical wizard Roy Wood, ELO have undergone several changes in their line-up, but have finally settled down into a well-knit unit of extremely talented musicians.

They set out to experiment with the use of strings and bring some classical influence into a rock 'n' roll format.

ELO have, over the past year or so, become giants in the recording field. Their LP, "A New World Record" – which was their fourth "gold" album in a row – firmly established them as a unique band offering a very different sound.

Their last concert tour of the United States was a "sell out". They have been accused (if accusation is the right word) of not only entertaining their audiences, but also educating them. Which can't be a bad thing when you think about it!

Unlike many other English rock groups who feel they have to be violent in order to be noticed, the ELO boys do not go around smashing up hotel rooms, throwing TV sets out of windows, or causing a public nuisance. All this is totally unnecessary and uncivilised.

Lynne, who is songwriter as well as guitarist and vocalist, says he does not base any of his songs on his own experiences. "I cannot relate to reality at all when it comes to writing songs. I always write purely fictional stuff."

There is an amusing story – absolutely true – told about the group's first record album. A United Artists recording executive in the USA told his secretary to call Don Arden (ELO's manager since they were first formed) in England and get the title of the new ELO album. She left a note on his desk, saying she had phoned – no answer! Her boss rather foolishly took this as the title, and the group's first album was issued under the title "No Answer", much to the bewilderment of Don Arden and the group back in Britain.

It was a song from their second album, "ELO 11", however, which really saw the group "take off". This was ELO's rendition of the Chuck Berry classic "Roll Over Beethoven".

"It was the most obvious idea in the world," says drummer Bev Bevan, "to start with a portion of Beethoven's Fifth Symphony and then go into 'Roll Over Beethoven' – but no one had ever done it before. It became our first big hit." This piece is still one of the highlights of ELO's stage concerts.

BE BOP DELUXE

Billy Nelson has been acclaimed by music critics as one of the best solo guitarists in the business. But this he casually shrugs off with the modest air of a Northern bloke who simply wants recognition more for his group than for himself.

The group he formed was BE BOP DELUXE, who finally broke through into the British single charts in 1976 with "Ships In The Night".

This public acceptance as a serious rock band was the culmination of a personal ambition Billy had kept to himself for some years.

Born in Wakefield, Yorkshire, he still prefers the quiet Northern country life to the hustle and bustle of London and Tin Pan Alley.

He first started out as a solo artist in 1972, making an album on his own called "Northern Dream", which he even ambitiously released on his own record label. Somehow, the record came into the hands of an executive from the giant EMI organisation. Billy was summoned to see them – and he arrived on their doorstep laden with tapes made by the new group he'd formed, Be Bop Deluxe.

Billy, and the group, were immediately signed up by EMI.

Unlike most other group leaders, Billy Nelson is not, he admits, very impressed with America. After touring the States with the band (a tour which was extended by three weeks because of their popularity) Billy returned home to write the album "Modern Music", which was greatly influenced by his experiences in America.

"I didn't like America very much," he says. "For me, it holds little glamour. The title track on the 'Modern Music' album reflects exactly how I felt . . . everyone racing about, on foot, by car, on planes. There's an instrumental track, with American sound effects, cars, guns going off, giving an overall impression of speed."

That album, incidentally, brought Be Bop many more fans.

On the Road... with David Essex

By Pauline McLeod, Pop Music Columnist, "Daily Mirror"

The cherry red Range Rover was slammed into reverse gear, backed up over the pavement and inched towards the stage door.

The engine was left ticking over as the last chords of the encore crept out into the cold night air.

Inside the converted cinema 1,500 kids were yelling, stomping and screaming for more. David Essex took his cue from their cries and ran. No time to change. No time for anything, except grab a towel and get the hell out of there.

He dived into the back of the Rover and as the fans clawed at the window pane, he sank into his seat – totally wiped out.

He looked over his shoulder towards the Gaumont Cinema, Doncaster, where he'd shared the bill with "Night of the Bloody Apes" showing in the adjoining hall, and then settled down for the five-minute race back to his hotel . . . and safety. The first night of the biggest British tour ever undertaken was just a few minutes behind him.

But every night of the six-week tour was different. And the "get-in" and "get-out" points of each gig (among the most crucial moments for any rock idol who is likely to be torn limb from limb if he is left to his fans for a few minutes!) were handled with care, caution and a great deal of speed by Bev Bush, younger brother of promoter Mel Bush.

Life on the road with the David Essex touring company is a bit like being at a very long party – the fun never stops. Although it's always possible that those people directly responsible to Essex, now in his 30s, may tell a different story.

For he is meticulous, precise and demanding in his requirements of his band and road crew, to the point of perfection.

As one of the crew put it: "He knows exactly what he wants and expects to get it, no matter what extra hours it means we have to put in. However, it is preferable to work for somebody who is decisive and knows what directives to give us."

And Essex, backed by one of the finest set of musicians around, was for ever pushing the band to get into the action up front. Basically musicians and not performers, they found it difficult to relax before a seething mass of teenagers who looked more like a Rent-a-Riot crowd than a concert audience.

As the tour moved to the larger cities and towards the south of England, so the girls became more determined to grab at least a momentary hold on their hero. And David's bodyguards became more determined that they didn't!

Their approach to security is novel. Gone are the days when David would leave a theatre dressed as a policeman or a plumber or be carried off in a freight container.

Mel Bush relies solely on their convoy of three Range Rovers, each one stripped of every piece of identification except the number plates (and there's a spare set of those) and capable of going anywhere undetected.

"We can usually get him out of the theatre without him having to step more than a few feet to the vehicle," said Mel.

Once off the stage the showman in David disappears and he becomes one of the lads again. The "gang" gather in the hotel bar to decide where to spend their off-duty time.

And David is like the Pied Piper – they all want to follow him. As often or not nobody did very much, except go to a club for an hour.

For me, going out with the Essex mob en masse was like being the odd one out at a stag party.

"We're never bothered by groupies, we don't seem to be that sort of band," said Essex. And it's true. During four days on the road with them there was a remarkable lack of female company.

"I have never been the wild bachelor type. The kids realise that, I'm sure. I've never hidden the fact that I'm married, with children.

"Of course we all miss each other when I'm away, but Maureen is very understanding. She realises that touring is what I have to do."

That he is a fairly reluctant sex symbol there is no doubt. But there's no hiding it, he'd have half the country's teenagers fawning at his feet if he gave them so much as a wink. Instead, he goes out of his way not to be provocative.

Maybe he's got his manager to blame for his fame and fortune. Derek Bowman saw the potential in Essex when he was just seventeen. Within three months he'd changed the name Cook to Essex . . . and the show was on the road. How did Bowman decide on the name?

"Well, he came from Essex, it sounded right for the rock world and for the theatre and it had "sex" in it. It was just what he needed," says Bowman.

Yes, the working-class superstar has come a long way since he went for his first theatre audition for a musical in Paignton at the age of nineteen.

On his opening night there were only 13 people in the audience . . . and one of those was his manager!

David Essex, during a break in rehearsals, for Top of the Pops, with (left to right) Robin Nash, the producer, and Stan Appel, the TV director.

SHOTS FROM THE SHOW

Our roving camerman gets some offbeat shots during rehearsals for TV's No. 1 pop show. . . .

Putting the show on the screen. . . . This is the scene in the director's gallery at TV Centre when Top of the Pops is produced. Left to right: Robin Nash, the producer, Angela Wilson, the vision-mixer, and Stan Appel, who directs the programme.

Jimmy Savile, limbering up during a break in the show.

Steve Harley of Cockney Rebel, on the stand.

Wow! What a smashing set of legs! The dancing girls who add glamour to the show every week . . . Legs & Co.

Pussycat, belting out a hit song.

Little Tina Charles in action.

The lovely Kiki Dee.

Guys 'n' Dolls . . . getting the act right in a rehearsal session.

Billy Ocean . . . playing up to the cameras.

It's the West Coast Sound...

By Bob Hart, Record Columnist, "The Sun"

Some people say it's the weather. Others say it is the influence of the Pacific Ocean which laps at the coast of California. But everybody agrees that SOMETHING makes the music of America's West Coast very, very special.

It all started back in the Sixties with bands like The Byrds and Buffalo Springfield. The Byrds were as important to the development of American pop music as the Beatles were to what was going on in Britain.

Buffalo Springfield had a short, spectacular career, with perhaps their most important contribution being the bands that sprung from their ashes – bands like Crosby, Stills, Nash and Young, Loggins and Messina and Poco.

It was CSN & Y that pushed the West Coast most firmly back into the British charts. Their close-harmony singing and the country feel to much of their music established the pattern for much of the West Coast music that has followed.

Few singles from West Coast performers found their way into the British charts early in the Seventies – with CSN & Y and Joni Mitchell providing the occasional exception to the rule.

But now, in the second half of the Seventies, the floodgates have opened. British pop fans have rediscovered the West Coast. And we seem to like some of the West Coast superstars even more than American pop fans do.

We love the first lady of West Coast music, *Linda Ronstadt*. Ever since she first appeared in Britain late in 1976 she has had an enormous and highly excited following in this country. With very good reason, of course. Because Linda is sensational.

As her music would suggest, Linda is a country girl. She grew up in Tucson, Arizona, to the sound of country music being sung and played by her father, and being pumped out of the radio 24 hours a day.

She moved to Los Angeles when she was 18 and made a number of false starts before shooting to the top of the American charts with an album, and a single, called "Heart Like A Wheel" in 1975.

But superb as her records inevitably are, fully to understand the magic of Linda Ronstadt you must see her in action. Standing in the middle of a stage in her well-worn jeans and flimsy top that reveals a trim, tanned midriff. Wrapping her pure, powerful voice around songs that link her country roots to her role as a Seventies rock idol.

I first met Linda shortly before a concert in Philadelphia, and she told me: "Nobody in the world gets as nervous as me before a concert. Honestly, I suffer from terminal stage fright.

"I have been singing for nearly 15 years, but instead of things getting easier as the years go by, they seem to get harder."

But to see Linda in action, you would never know. She seldom moves from behind that central microphone stand, except occasionally to chat to a musician at the end of a song. She seems as meek as a mouse when she introduces a song, but there is nothing meek about the voice that rings through the auditorium when she is singing.

Linda told me: "When you come from a place like Tucson, and you leave home to try to make your way in the music business when you are still an innocent kid, you are sure to have problems. It puts you right in line for some pretty hard knocks, and I had my share.

"The biggest single danger is that you will lose your nerve. It happens when you get hurt so badly by something or somebody that you stop believing in yourself.

Linda Ronstadt

Glenn Frey

"My confidence was sabotaged by being on the road with bands that weren't right. Playing with sound systems that didn't work. And being paid almost nothing for my trouble and heartache.

"I had a string of managers before I learned how to tell the good ones from the bad ones. The ones who want you to make it from the ones who just want to take all they can get and leave you on a junk pile somewhere. Things like that held up my musical development, but I learnt in the end. The hard way, I suppose.

"And now I feel strong. I feel strong for having survived 15 very confused years of wondering what was going to happen to me next. Of floating around and being too insecure to form a close relationship with anybody.

"But now things are working out. I feel great because I am working, my music is better than it has ever been, I am still healthy, and still relatively sane after all I went through. Success is important, of course. But being in one piece and able to enjoy your success is much more important."

A singer as good as Linda needs some very special musicians on stage with her. People whose command of their instruments can match her own virtuosity. And she usually finds them.

The trouble is, Linda finds people so good that it is inevitable that sooner or later her backing musicians will make it in their own right and she will have to start looking all over again.

And that's where the West Coast supergroup *The Eagles* came from – behind Linda Ronstadt. They were her backing group until record company bosses saw the possibilities, and now they have established themselves as the logical successors to CSN & Y.

"Take It Easy" and "Lyin' Eyes" were the two monster hits that established them in Britain. And now they are among our top ten favourite bands.

These days, The Eagles are Glenn Frey and Don Henley – the two central figures of the band – Joe Walsh, Don Felder and Randy Meisner. They are all superb musicians, but it is their close-harmony vocals that have set them apart. They have carried on in the CSN & Y tradition, and built on it. Improved on the masters.

As Frey says: "Clearly, they were our strongest influence. And I think the fact that they dissolved so rapidly was an enormous disappointment to us all. A disappointment and a warning – because it increased our determination to stay together and battle through the problems that exist in this business."

Don Henley says: "We are survivors. We all intend to keep our heads. To be around to enjoy the fruits of our labours. Rather than fold under the pressure of the business, we try to harness it. We all play and write very well under pressure."

As with most of the top West Coast bands, none of the Eagles actually come from California. Henley came from Texas and Frey came from Detroit. The band got together when they met up in Los Angeles and found their dreams and ideas coincided.

One of the few home-grown Californians to make his mark in West Coast music is *Andrew Gold* – another musician who first came to most people's attention as a backing musician for Linda Ronstadt.

It took just two albums and a couple of hit singles for Andrew

The Eagles

Andrew Gold

to prove that he can stand on his own two feet, which is precisely what he is doing now – with a devoted following of British fans ready to snap up any material he records.

And while many of the traditionally "laid-back" West Coast heroes claim to detest the idea of stardom and everything that goes with it, Andrew happily admits that the bright lights attract him.

He says: "I love the idea of stardom. I would love it all. I grew up in Hollywood in a showbiz family, and I suppose that helps. I always wanted to be a film star. Not an actor, just a star. And I suppose that is still my secret dream."

Andrew's father, Ernest, composes film music. His greatest success was with the music for "Exodus". And Andrew's mother, Marnie Nixon, provides the singing voice for film actresses who can't quite measure up in that department – like Natalie Wood in "West Side Story" and Audrey Hepburn in "My Fair Lady".

Andrew said: "My parents have never done anything to discourage me from going into showbiz. They never wanted me to be a lawyer or a doctor or anything like that."

Less enthralled than Andrew by the idea of stardom – but quicker to find it – is *Jackson Browne*. He began to influence West Coast thinking early in the Seventies with his beautiful songs which everybody wanted to sing. And his first success as a writer came when he co-wrote the first Eagles hit, "Take It Easy".

It took until 1976 for British fans to discover him, but now we are making up for lost time. His albums are seldom out of the charts, and rightly so. He is the most gentle and thoughtful of all the West Coast performers – with a pure vocal style and lilting melody lines that allow the power of his lyrics to sneak up on you.

He says: "I grew up in Los Angeles, but I wasn't born here. I did most of my listening to music here, though, and the effect of the West Coast on your musical ideas is an incredible thing.

"Some people find West Coast music bland. They say it all sounds the same. But they are simply not listening closely enough. There is a lot going on with a band like The Eagles – they are complete masters of a certain type of music.

"And there are very few songs being written on the West Coast these days that don't have something to say."

The ladies have always played an important part in West Coast music. *Joni Mitchell* was the first female superstar to emerge, and her songs are still among the most interesting and original being written anywhere in the world. Only Bob Dylan and Bruce Springsteen can live with Joni the lyricist.

Maria Mulduar is another enormous talent. Her "Midnight At The Oasis" hit, and the tour that followed it in 1976, established her in Britain. And she has shown that she can turn out light, sexy and beautifully sung songs that nobody can better.

But perhaps the best is yet to come. My own favourite of the West Coast ladies is the bubbling, freckle-faced *Bonnie Raitt*. She writes superb songs, sings them in a voice not unlike Linda Ronstadt's, and is a superb guitarist. She already has a growing following in Britain, and by the end of the Seventies could be challenging Linda and Joni for the top spot.

But whoever is on top, the one thing we can be sure of is that West Coast music will be affecting our lives for years to come. The Hollywood dream factory that once shaped our tastes in films has now been largely replaced by the Hollywood musical factory.

In Los Angeles, people eat, sleep and live their music. It surrounds them. In every bar there seems to be a potential superstar just waiting to be heard. And British rock fans, at long last, are ready to listen.

Joni Mitchell

FRAMPTON MARLEY & MERCURY THEY'RE MAGIC!

By Bob Hart

Everybody loves a star. Especially a gold-plated, diamond-studded superstar. And the pop world has turned out more than its share of them.

There was Sinatra in the Forties, Presley in the Fifties, all four Beatles and Rolling Stone Mick Jagger in the Sixties.

But who will be remembered as the superstars of the Seventies? Elton John, probably. But as the Seventies draw to a close, there are three men who might just challenge Elton's supremacy in the final analysis.

For Elton has retired from the touring circuit. He wants to sit back and think about life, watch football and make his music in recording studios. He is dropping out of the spotlight.

Will that allow a pretender to snatch the glory away from him in the last couple of years of the Seventies? Will America's top contender Bruce Springsteen free himself of his legal shackles and do what so many critics have said he would do?

Possibly. As a devout Springsteen fan, I sincerely hope he is allowed to realise his full potential before the Seventies draw to a close. But at the same time, I see three other performers capable of making just as big an impact if they get the breaks.

They are British-born blonde bombshell *Peter Frampton*, Jamaica's Black Prince of Reggae, *Bob Marley*, and that exotic front man of our newest Supergroup, Queen's *Freddie Mercury*.

All are giant talents. All are made of genuine, 24-carat superstar material. And all have that strange, elusive, inaccessible quality that is essential to the real superstar.

First Frampton. He is a rock veteran, of course, having hit a few of the highspots in the Sixties and early Seventies with The Herd and Humble Pie. But Peter Frampton, solo superstar singer and guitarist, is a product of the Seventies.

He looks like a million dollars, which is roughly what he earns in a good quarter. That bubbling blonde hair, those clear blue eyes and those perfect features looking as though they would be enough to set him up for some kind of stardom even without his musical talent.

But musical talent he most certainly has. He is a fine guitarist, a strong singer, and a very good writer. He also knows a thing or two about leading a band from the front, and piecing together a really gripping rock concert.

Until he finally smashed to the top of the charts in 1976, Peter had spent some five years plugging away in America, playing clubs, supporting successful bands. And usually losing money. He put out four albums that did moderately well, but no more than that. And gradually he built up a following that everybody – including Peter – assumed was small, if fanatical. It wasn't until the incredible Frampton Comes Alive album hit the shops in mid '76 that everybody learned the truth.

Peter says: "It took me five years to be an overnight success. What a crazy business this is! When the album hit the shops I was £50,000 in debt, and seriously considering taking a steady job as a session musician. But within six months I was being told by my accountants that I should go out and spend as much money as I could or else the taxman would take it. Amazing!

"But I'm glad it took a while. If the first album I made in America had been a success, I would probably have ended up in a loony bin. I had no confidence

Peter Frampton

when I was on stage in those days, and not much confidence off-stage. When I was in The Herd, we had hits, and we were on Top of the Pops. But those were the days when everybody screamed and nobody listened. It was all a giggle.

"In Humble Pie, I was just the guitarist. All the attention was on Stevie Marriott, and it was easy for me. But then when I came to America I forced myself to be the front man. I went out on my own.

"America is a great country in which to learn all you need to know about this business. I have watched everybody. Learning all the time. And stealing bits from the masters on occasions. Now I can play to a crowd of 50,000 or so and feel confident. Stunned, but confident.

"I have to spend a lot of my time on the road now, but I don't mind that. I have had plenty of training for it over the years. I love touring places like Japan and Australia. But most of all I love going back to Britain. I suppose I have lived out every exile's dream. I have been able to go home after years away and I have gone home victorious. A winner. It feels fantastic."

Bob Marley is a very different style of superstar. He is a mystical, mysterious man. But the real Marley magic is in his irresistible reggae music, and the way he delivers it from a stage. There is only one Marley.

The gleaming, copper-coloured skin of his face is stretched over finely-boned features. Sausage-shaped rolls of woolly hair bounce wildly as he leaps, dances and jogs around the stage. The guitar slung across his body is little more than a prop – the words are the thing, and he sings them as though he means them.

Comparison with Jagger is inevitable. Like Jagger, he is one of those rare creatures who can mesmerise an audience. While Marley is on stage, you can't look away. The warmth and subdued power of his music – pumped out behind him by the incredible Wailers – takes hold of an audience more forcefully than anything I have ever encountered. Marley just grinned when I asked him how he did it.

He said: "That's the positive vibrations, man. That's what makes it work. That's reggae music. You can't look away because it's real. You listen to what I sing because I mean what I sing. There's no secret, man. No big deal. Just honesty, that's all."

Marley is a gentle, philosophical man. His father was a British army officer, his mother was Jamaican. And Bob grew up in Kingston's trenchtown area – the Jamaican capital's shameful human garbage dump. His brilliant lyrics are often compared with the words of another rock prophet, Bob Dylan. Some of his sentiments are violent and revolutionary. He is an angry man. But Marley is also a man of peace. Violence, to him, is for putting into songs. Not into practice.

Britain was the first country outside of Jamaica to pick up on the magic of Marley. Wailers records were shipped into Britain to be sold to the Jamaican population, but many of them found their way into white hands. And young white rock fans liked what they heard.

Stardom has not spoiled Marley. He hardly seems aware of it. He said: "Money doesn't matter. Only music matters. When people think first about the money and then about the music, the music won't be worth the money they were thinking about."

Marley's music first found its way into the British charts without most people realising that he was involved. He wrote a song called "I Shot The Sheriff", and Eric Clapton's version of it was a massive hit.

But these days Marley has his hits in his own name. Nobody who has ever seen or heard Marley can ever forget his music, and his magic could easily make him the biggest black rock star of them all.

More than Marley, and even more than Frampton, *Freddie Mercury* comes close to being in the classic mould of British superstars.

Like Jagger, Freddie, the brilliant front-man of that supergroup Queen, has off-beat looks. Jagger has those pneumatic lips, and Freddie has the most prominent set of front teeth ever to have found their way onto a pop fan's wall.

But behind those teeth are dark, exotic good looks of the kind that make stars into superstars. And Freddie's musical and vocal talents are enormous.

With a true superstar, lifestyle is important. And Freddie lives out most of our fantasies for us with more style than we could ever manage to live them for ourselves. Even if we did have Freddie's kind of money.

I once joined Freddie for tea in the suite of his hotel. His New York hotel, of course. And it was the Royal Suite, naturally.

Queen had played yet another triumphant New York concert the night before, and Freddie was still feeling the effects of it. Warm tea was allowed to slide down Mr. Mercury's regal throat as he prodded gingerly at some bruises on the side of his neck.

He explained: "My very enjoyable and highly promising career very nearly came to an untimely end last night. Two young girls outside the hotel decided to claim my scarf as a souvenir. Unfortunately, they ignored the fact that it was wrapped around my neck at the time, and they almost strangled me.

"I'm sure Her Majesty doesn't have to suffer that sort of indignity. But then, she hasn't got anything in the charts at the moment, has she?"

Freddie's dress sense is sensational. He never looks less than spectacular, and he is not the sort of chap who believes in going unnoticed. Satin seems to be his favourite fabric, with silk coming a close second. And he loves those loose, floppy, Japanese-style jackets.

But as he is quick to point out: "There is a quiet side to me too, you know. My home life is a very civilised affair, and I hardly ever dress up to watch the television. Unless I'm watching a Royal occasion, of course."

Freddie lives in a splendid London flat with his girlfriend, Mary Austin. And there, he has even been known to wear nothing more exotic than a pair of faded jeans and a T-shirt, which makes a change from the membrane-thin ballet costume he wears to bound around the stage.

But Freddie decided that there were better things to do in the city of New York than sit around sipping tea and discussing sartorial matters. He suggested that we should tour the shops, and it seemed a reasonable suggestion.

It seemed a slightly less reasonable suggestion an hour later when an ugly crowd of burly housewives were gathering while Freddie insisted that the manicurist demonstrating lacquers in Macey's Department Store should paint his fingernails black.

He clucked: "But only the ones on the left hand, dear. I NEVER wear nail polish on the right hand."

Twenty minutes later he was insisting that I invest in some "stunning, and most reasonable" glitter shoes. GREEN glitter shoes. I declined.

The trouble is, you have to be a superstar to get away with wearing shoes like that. And it is just possible that Freddie could be wearing them for quite a few years.

For in the final analysis, I suspect it will be Freddie Mercury who finishes first in the race for the King of the Seventies Superstars title. But what a race . . .

Freddie Mercury, with his group Queen

Frampton
ueen

BOB MARLEY

When it comes to reggae music, there is no doubt at all about the world's No. 1 master. His name is Bob Marley. And his group is The Wailers.

Marley, based in Jamaica, West Indies, has been making records since way back in 1962. He's produced a countless string of hits. But he finally burst through, in 1976, to become the uncrowned international King of Reggae in America with the stunning album "Rastaman Vibration".

His records are now fairly guaranteed gold discs even before they are released. The advance orders in the United States for "Rastaman Vibration" totalled more than a million dollars in hard cash, helped by the fact that Marley and The Wailers went on an extensive tour of the US.

His concerts in this country have invariably been instant sell-outs.

Abba

No group, or solo artist, owes more to the much maligned Eurovision Song Contest than Abba, the attractive "doubles partnership" from Sweden.

For although they were a well-known and popular group in their country prior to 1974, they were unheard of in Britain before they came over to represent Sweden in the Euro Song Contest mounted by the BBC at Brighton.

And even when they won the contest – with the bouncy and foot-tapping song "Waterloo" – few critics thought they would survive the tough hurly-burly of the Big Time.

But Abba proved everyone wrong. In fact, from the battle of Waterloo they stormed on to conquer the world. Thanks to very careful planning, and a constant eye to the commercial record market, Abba have now become a truly international group.

The group is made up of Agnetha (known as Anna), her husband Bjorn, Benny and the lady he lives with, Annifrid (known as Frida). Hence their Christian name initials form the name of the group.

They first got together as a vocal group in the early 1970s. Before that, Benny started out with a Beatle-like group in Sweden called The Hep Stars. He met Bjorn, in 1966, and they teamed up in a folk group, The Hootenanny Singers.

Anna became one of Sweden's top girl singers after a solo hit record, in 1968, "I Was So In Love". And Frida made her breakthrough around the same time in a Swedish TV series called "Hyland's Corner".

For the last four years, however, Abba have really taken off! They've been, without a doubt, the most consistently commercial pure pop group in Europe.

Cleverly, they have acquired the musical ability to capture audiences of all tastes and all ages. They have had hit records in practically every known record chart.

Their "Greatest Hits" album, released in 1976, brought them a platinum disc. And before that, their albums "Waterloo" and "Abba" both earned silver records.

They then added to their collection of silver and gold discs with a string of hit singles, including "Mamma Mia", "Fernando", and "Dancing Queen".

The single, "Dancing Queen", broke all records by racing to the No. 1 spot in our charts and passed the gold mark with more than 500,000 British sales within a month!

They certainly seem to have discovered the magic formula for pop success right across the board.

Even away from the bright lights of show business, this happy-go-lucky foursome hit all the right notes together. Anna and Bjorn live only a short distance from Frida and Benny, in a suburb of Stockholm. And they even spend their summer holidays together – usually "messing about in boats", because all four are very keen sailors.

Wings

When Paul McCartney finally split up from the Beatles – amid much legal wrangling and some personal slanging matches – few could have predicted that he would ever be as great again, in musical terms, with any other group.

But Paul proved everyone wrong, when he formed his new group Wings. After a few years in the wilderness, he came back – slowly at first, and with some signs of trepidation, for he was "feeling his way" very gently.

If any proof was needed that McCartney was really back in business, it was surely provided by Wings' mammoth world tour, which was spread over a 13-month period from 1975 to 1976.

When Wings went on tour – complete with two enormous articulated trucks full of electronic equipment, speakers, amplifiers, lights and musical instruments – it turned out to be one of the biggest roadshows in rock music history.

The group visited ten countries, and played to more than two million people.

The tour took in Britain, Australia, America, the Continent, Yugoslavia, and culminated in three fantastic concerts at the Empire Pool, Wembley.

When they hit America, they travelled throughout the tour in a chartered BAC one-eleven, which was specially fitted out inside like a sitting room, with luxurious armchairs and carpets and other "home-from-home comforts".

The band set up four bases – in New York, Dallas, Chicago and Los Angeles – from which they flew in for each night's gig.

This way, Paul and his group of musicians ensured a semblance of "home life" while on tour. They even took with them a complete games outfit – including a table tennis table, football game and darts board, for their leisure hours.

Back in Europe, Wings were invited by UNESCO to play to an audience in St. Mark's Square, Venice, to raise money to help save the city from sinking into the sea.

The tour was a complete "sell out" all the way across the world. The group (Paul, his wife Linda, Denny Laine, Jimmy McCulloch, and Joe English) had never experienced anything like this before in terms of audience satisfaction.

And for Paul himself, the personal satisfaction he gained on the tour gave him more of a thrill than anything he'd ever experienced even in the heyday of the famous Beatles.

For Paul, this was a personal way of announcing to the world: "I'm back!" And he's still, remarkably, as popular as ever.

JETHRO TULL

Few bands have done more to put Britain on the map, worldwise, in the music scene, than Jethro Tull.

They've now been going for ten years, with never a sign of their success waning.

Over the years, they've scored with an impressive list of hit records (ten gold albums on the trot, for starters), even though the line-up of the band has changed from time to time.

Ian Anderson is the only founder member still with the group. To all intents and purposes, Ian has now become *the* Jethro Tull.

He first came down from the North in search of fame and fortune in London, with another band. But when this broke up, he formed Jethro Tull, in 1968.

Originally, their early music was a mixture of jazz, blues and rock. But over the years, Anderson's bizarre influence has taken them into other realms of music.

It was Anderson's eccentric behaviour on stage, as much as the music, which was responsible for the success of the group.

Hopping on one leg in maniac fashion, dressed in a tattered raincoat, his rat's-tail hair hanging over his shoulders, he brought an element of whimsy and amusement to their music. He was variously described as a "mad-dog Fagin", a "demented dancing master", a "deranged flamingo."

He boldly introduced the flute to his musical repertoire – and immediately created a new sound, and a new image, for the Jethro Tull band.

They are so highly original, that no other band has ever had the audacity to dare to imitate them. If you want Tull music, as someone once said, there's still only one place to get it – from Anderson, the superb showman, and Co.

The secret of their whole success seems to be that Anderson and the Jethro Tull boys really do believe in enjoying what they do. "I'm probably one of the few musicians you'll ever meet who isn't jaded about music," says Ian.

"From a very personal point of view, I want to justify that line on my passport which describes my occupation as: Musician."

A few years back, Jethro Tull controversially announced their retirement from the concert circuit. They took the band off the road and spent a year in self-imposed exile abroad, mostly in Switzerland.

Inevitably, of course, they couldn't stay away for long. They were soon back, touring America and Britain, and increasing their mammoth record sales.

But they did have a five-year lay-off on TV, until early 1976. Then they came back with a vociferous bang.

Says Ian Anderson: "I was delighted when bands like ours were invited to appear on 'Top of the Pops' and other TV shows. I am totally unafraid of doing television and can only hope that other bands like us will follow, instead of turning down appearances on the box. To be invited to perform on TV is a great opportunity, and the responsibility is with the artist to make the best of it."

Certainly, while Jethro Tull are around, there can be no lack of entertainment and Fun – with a capital F!

Bay City Rollers

The Rollers – On Tour in America

By Matthew Ellis

Big Paddy Callaghan – broad as a house and twice as tough – has minded the biggest and the best in the world of pop and rock music.

"Minding" needs little explanation. Paddy is the human armour plating that stands between the elite of pop and the over-enthusiastic fans, especially those who swarm around when the top groups are on tour.

He's jumped into the cauldron of fame with most of the real hysteria-detonators: Gary Glitter, The Osmonds, David Cassidy . . .

But in Paddy's book there is one band which triggers a wilder reaction than any other – "I promise you, mate," he says, "in my experience there's never been anything like this lot."

Who? You've guessed, of course. The Bay City Rollers are still the hottest property around when it comes to crowd reaction.

The fortunes of the group in the maxi-profit area of records may shrink and swell a little now. No longer can the name on the label guarantee a major chart hit. No more are their albums automatic additions to the pop fan's disc-list.

But a live performance by the Rollers is still an event that will bring cold sweat to the brows of the local police, worried frowns to the staffs of the theatres in which the band plays, and a contented, affluent smile to the face of Tam Paton, manager of the most potent teenybopper draw in the business.

Paddy Callaghan, upon whose barn-like shoulders the safety of the Rollers depends, has the knack of remaining placid and cool at all times. Well, most of the time!

In Boston, Massachusetts, during the tour which firmly established the group's enormous potential in the United States, a considerable crowd gathered outside the stage door, blocking the narrow passage to the waiting limousines.

A policewoman, blonde and pretty and with a revolver as big as a prize marrow nestling against her hip, smiled encouragingly as Eric Faulkner, Les McKeown and the other Rollers prepared to run the gauntlet. But, then, she was on the safe side of the door!

A flying column – spearheaded by two policemen, rearguarded by Paddy Callaghan, with the Rollers sandwiched between – went out into the evening air as though fired from a gun.

The column made all of seven or eight yards before splintering in all directions. The police disappeared under the first swell of eager bodies; the Rollers fought hard to retain balance, rising and falling like corks in an angry sea, and Paddy, his eyes for once clouding with concern, bravely plunged into the pandemonium to protect his charges.

Five minutes later the Rollers were in the limousines and edging clear of the crowd. Paddy, soaked in sweat, was gently consoling the more distraught fans. And the policemen? Well, the policemen, non-believers before, no doubt, were busy reclaiming their helmets and telling each other that never – never! – had Boston seen anything quite like this.

Back at the hotel, with the Rollers installed in the relative safety of their rooms and with a cold beer never far from his lips, Paddy Callaghan reflected: "That was a tough one. But there's been a lot worse than that, mate."

And Eric Faulkner later confirmed: "It was a bit hairy, but I wasn't frightened. After all, there was one occasion when we were trapped in an underground car park. That was really terrifying. And in Canada once so many fans climbed on to the roof of the car that it started to buckle. We weren't laughing too much then, I can tell you!"

"Yeah," said Paddy, "and it can be pretty bad in Japan, where the Rollers are the biggest thing *ever*, too . . ."

Paddy's work for the day was still not finished. Like a lonely vigilante, he would patrol the hotel corridor – escaping only now and then for a welcome beer, but always posting a deputy – ensuring that the over-devoted fan did not succumb to an urge of midnight door-knocking.

The pattern was repeated in most cities during that American tour. And in Britain the problems are, of course, far greater.

Paddy Callaghan has mixed views of the reaction by police departments to the visit by the Rollers to their towns.

"Some are great," he said, "but others just don't realise what they are in for. One police chief in England – no, I won't say where – got hold of me on the day of the concert and said, 'Don't interfere. We'll handle the fans'."

"I tried to give him some advice, but he didn't want to know. And when the fans started to go really potty he just didn't know what to do. Afterwards, when the local police lads looked as though they'd been dragged through a rugby scrum, he said to me, 'Why didn't you tell me what was going to happen'?

"'Well, mate', I told him, 'why didn't you ask'?"

The inhibitions forced upon the Rollers by the non-stop dedication of their fans are disturbing. What normal young man wants to live a life consisting only of aeroplanes, cars, theatres and hotel rooms? Who would be satisfied to visit some of the great cities of the world, yet see nothing but streets blurred by the speed of a limousine? And which fan would exchange his freedom of choice for a diet of food and entertainment restricted to meals from room service and the mind-numbing flicker of a television screen?

The Rollers have adjusted to this life remarkably well, but it is significant that Eric Faulkner was at one time depressed enough to take an overdose of drugs and that both Alan Longmuir and Ian Mitchell quit the group in 1976 because of increasing pressure and the curtailment of their personal freedom.

"The Rollers get absolutely worn out," said Tam Paton, nervous and tired himself towards the end of the American tour. "The pressures of the kind of life they lead are enormous – it's like being on a conveyor belt that you can't stop."

In Atlanta, Georgia, the band had a night off and, as they were not as well known in the south as in the north of the U.S.A., some of them decided to venture out of their hotel to a local restaurant. Les McKeown, "Woody" Wood and Derek Longmuir relaxed with members of the tour entourage and representatives of their record company – and it was remarkable to see them almost visibly shedding the tension that had built up over the previous few weeks.

No Roller drank anything stronger than Coke, nor did they eat much. But the atmosphere was easy, the conversation light and bright and funny. Only two or three waiters asked for autographs and there wasn't a scream to be heard.

Paddy Callaghan sat at the end of the table, beer to hand, enjoying the experience of seeing the Rollers enjoy themselves.

"I should think so, too," he said. "No matter how much money they earn, they don't get the chance to do this very often – they don't get much *fun*."

Two days later the Rollers finished their tour and took an early morning flight back to Britain. Even then the pressure was not fully relaxed; it's surprising the number of aeroplane passengers who want the autograph of a pop star, even if they are not quite sure which particular group they are asking.

"I'll be glad to get home," said Les McKeown.

"So will I," said Paddy Callaghan.

The Pick of my Pop

By Tim Ewbank

Every pop fan must know the feeling. That moment you come out of a theatre, club or dancehall after seeing a band and it's raining and the last bus has gone.

Yet you don't mind. And you don't even notice that your hands are stinging from the applause you have given and that your feet are like lead from non-stop dancing.

You don't mind any of it. Because you have enjoyed yourself.

For me there are three bands that will always send me home happy. Always put me in a good mood when they are on TV.

They are *Mud*, *Showaddywaddy*, and *The Rubettes*. Because all three work themselves to the bone to give their followers a good show as well as good records.

Their own enjoyment is infectious. That's not to say they are anything but professional, because the members of all three bands have served long apprenticeships as musicians before hitting the big time.

Take Dagenham-born John Richardson, drummer with *The Rubettes*. John spent eight years gaining experience in local bands. His free time was spent learning to sight-read music to enable him to do session work.

Today the study at his mock-Tudor house in Essex is piled high with Gold Discs the group have collected all over Europe and in England during the past few years.

But John is not one to rest on his laurels. I remember watching him closely on a frantic dash from a huge Paris concert to an airport for a flight back to England for another concert.

There was barely time to snatch anything to eat. But there was John at the airport restaurant, still practising with his drum sticks between mouthfuls of food and sips of coffee.

"We always set out to give our best to everyone who comes to see us, either live or on TV," says John.

"We strive for perfection. Perfection on record is terribly important, of course. But just as important is being able to reproduce our records perfectly on stage.

"Yet we never lose sight of enjoyment. We like playing and we want to be certain that our enjoyment comes over to the fans. If they go home without being able to say they have had a really good time, then we feel we have let them down."

The past year has been a vital one for The Rubettes. They established themselves as a four-piece band after gaining their biggest hits with a five-man line-up.

"Under One Roof" took them back into the charts and their next single "Baby I Know" became a hit and won them a lot of new fans. In addition they scored a success with an album of their own songs.

More importantly, they appeared before their British fans for the first time for nearly two years. The rest of the time they had spent performing to ecstatic fans on the Continent where they are treated like gods. Even the son of the French President signed them up to do a special performance for him.

"But our British following is dear to our hearts," John emphasises. "They always will be.

"We all get a kick out of seeing happy faces at our gigs, people dancing and clapping to the music. But we get an even bigger kick if those faces are British."

It's four years now since they rocketed to the top of the charts for the first time with "Sugar Baby Love". "Top of the Pops" did a lot for that record. It showed that here was a group who had stacks of musical ability, plenty of style, and a vital understanding that pop music is there to be enjoyed by both performers and audience.

The same can be said of *Showaddywaddy*. Originally they were two Leicester bands, The Choice and The Golden Hammers.

Whenever they were on the same bill they offered the manager a special extra for free: a joining together of their talents for a rollicking finale.

Singer Malcolm Allured remembers it well. "It soon got to the stage where what we were doing for free and for fun suddenly took off in a big way."

That's an understatement! They chalked up eight Top Ten hits in three years – without forgetting the fun side of their talents.

Every single one of the eight-man line-up has a genuine love of Fifties rock 'n' roll. And their performances showed it.

A buzz of excitement would grow to a crescendo at every venue they played as they took the stage. Out they would come with slicked-back hair, lurex shirts, lilac suits, white shoes and gum-chewing jaws. No wonder the fans went wild.

Each of them has eight suits costing £75 a time made in rock 'n' roll style. And what a fine sight they make as well as a fine sound.

Showaddywaddy have had several hits reviving top rock numbers. But we mustn't forget that they made their name with original hits like "Hey Rock and Roll", "Rock And Roll Lady", and "Hey Mr. Christmas".

Ask them about their music and they all reply: "We're proud of what we do. We have a great time on stage and we try and impart this to the audience."

There is no doubt that they do. Just like the third group in my *fun*tastic trio – *Mud*.

And there is equally no doubt that their name is never mud with the fans who go to see them. Because they give terrific value.

The group proved it last year by taking rock into the northern clubs, plugging in their amplifiers, and socking it to fans of all ages.

Wherever they play Mud get "Tiger Feet" twinkling, hands clapping, and audiences going wild until the fans are grateful when the group come up with "Lean On Me".

You can't help enjoying yourself with Mud. Remember when they wore imitation Tiger Feet for their big hit of the same name?

Les Gray, the group's friendly lead singer, says: "We hope we always give audiences what they want. And there is no chance of us ever becoming too clever for them.

"We're straight, simple, clear, direct. Just take us as you see and hear us."

Millions of fans have done just that – to the tune of a dozen hits.

Part of the group's appeal can be attributed to their musical grounding. Before they hit the big time they roared up and down Britain's motorways taking any gigs going.

The swishest deb parties in Surrey's stockbroker belt, discos in Glasgow, clubs in Coventry, ballrooms in Birmingham – you name them and Mud played them.

How did they hit upon their name? "Well," says Les, "we began rather cleverly. We called ourselves Mud because it had only three letters. That meant the name would look big even on the smallest posters!"

They need not have worried. Their bubbling enthusiasm for their music was bound to see them through.

The Rubettes, Showaddywaddy, Mud – three groups who in years to come will be able to put their hands on their hearts and truthfully say they brightened up the pop music scene. Without gimmicks, without sacrificing their musical ability. Nearly 30 massive hits between them is ample proof of that.

And doubtless there will be plenty more hits to come before they all hang up their guitars.

Showaddywaddy

In four years, the very visual Showaddywaddy band have done more for pure old-fashioned rock 'n' roll than any other group on the British scene.

They were unknown before they appeared on ITV's "New Faces". But they won much more than merely a talent show when they were adjudged the winners. For since then, Showaddywaddy have established themselves as one of the front-running groups in the rock 'n' roll field.

And why? Because fun is the name of their game. They've managed to inject more laughs, more thrills, more scintillating big-beat power into their performances than any other band around.

They've been acclaimed, unquestionably, the British Kings of Jive!

The Trocadero was a chain of Northern dance halls in the 1950s, and it was down at the Old Troc that the lads who now make up Showaddywaddy first became infatuated and electrified with the sound of rock 'n' roll.

In 1976, the lads issued their own album, titled "Trocadero", as something of a memento of those early teenage days they spent at the Troc dance halls.

They have since produced a string of hit records – both singles and albums – which have resulted in a collection of gold discs.

But they're a band who don't simply believe in sitting back and counting their record sales. They are constantly on tour in gigs all over the place. And over the last year they've also made it really big on record in Germany, Belgium, Holland, Scandinavia, Australia and New Zealand.

Gallagher & Lyle

Those two happy-go-lucky Scotsmen Benny Gallagher and Graham Lyle spent a number of years becoming slowly frustrated because their music did not receive wider commercial acclaim.

Then, in 1976, they made the important breakthrough with the hit single "Heart On My Sleeve". And suddenly – wham! They found themselves in great demand.

They first got together in the 1960s, playing with bands around their home town of Largs. Then they signed up with Apple Records, and started writing songs for such artists as Mary Hopkin, before moving on to join the McGuinness Flint band, where as songwriters they produced the hit numbers "When I'm Dead And Gone" and "Malt and Barley Blues".

They were always predominantly songwriters rather than performers. "The songwriting hasn't become less important to us," says Graham. "But the treatment of it has become much more important. You can never build a band up and make it dictate the musical material. The material has got to dictate to the band, or else the band isn't successful. All you get is a load of self-indulgence. There's no real place it's going."

Gallagher and Lyle have now become prolific song-spinners. For their album "Breakaway" (the title song of which scored a worldwide hit for Art Garfunkel) the boys wrote 30 numbers over a four month period, before recording. They then spent another month rehearsing with the band before selecting the final ten tracks for the LP.

The album lived up to its name for Gallagher and Lyle. This really was the big breakaway for the Scots couple.

After this album, they got together a band, and went on the road. They had huge chart success with the hit singles "I Wanna Stay With You" and "Heart On My Sleeve".

PAUL NICHOLAS

Reaching out for Stardom!

By Ken Irwin

From playing Jesus Christ Superstar, matinees and evenings, to Pop Superstar – that's the remarkable story of Paul Nicholas.

Within the last year or so, he has shot from run-of-the-mill working actor to become one of the most popular artists around in the pop field.

His career has turned full circle, for Paul started out as a rock 'n' roll singer at the age of 17. But it took him 13 years to make it as a singer in the pop charts.

"I'm glad it happened that way. Because I'm sure that if I'd found success in the pop world when I was just a teenager, I would not have been able to handle it," says Paul.

Despite his youthful looks, he's now in his early 30s. Just the right age, he feels, to fully appreciate exactly what has happened to him in his showbiz career.

He started out in a solicitor's office, working for his father when he was 16. "I wasn't very academic. I didn't get any 'O' levels or anything like that at school, and I didn't know what I wanted to do," recalls Paul.

"I hated working in the solicitor's office. I spent all my time serving writs on people. It was all very boring. It's not easy working for your father, even if you like the job. When you don't like the job, it's even worse.

"So I quit my job, learned to play the piano, and joined up with one or two bands, playing rock 'n' roll around London."

He made his professional debut, in fact, with Screaming Lord Sutch's group The Savages. "I used to peroxide my hair and grease it like they did in those old movies. And I wore a leopard skin, just like Tarzan. When I think of it now, it makes me squirm," says Paul.

"I gave it up when I was 20 because I got fed up playing with bands, and having very little success. So I went to work for a music publisher."

And that, as it turned out, was the best thing he ever did. Because this led to him going for an audition for the stage musical "Hair" . . . and Paul walked away with the leading role in what turned out to be a highly successful and original show, even though it was condemned by many as "shocking and depraved".

That was back in 1969. "It was my first big break," says Paul. "But 'Hair' was considered obscene by many people, because the cast stripped off on stage. And a few even appeared starkers.

"I was the only one who didn't actually have to take my clothes off in that show," he smiles. "I sat in the middle of it all. But I suppose that if I'd been asked to strip, I would have done. I probably would have been very nervous at first. But after you've done it once, it's like everything else. It becomes easier."

Paul stayed with the show for two years, and then later became its artistic director.

His next big break was the lead in another London West End musical, "Jesus Christ Superstar". "That was a real experience," he says. "It wasn't as much fun as appearing in 'Hair', because the part of Jesus was written fairly straight. I did get crucified every night. And the most awkward thing of all about that show was actually being put up on the cross.

"The first time I was on the cross, I actually cried. The piece of music was so sad. But I don't know why I cried. I felt very embarrassed about it afterwards. I was crying from exhaustion as much as anything else, I suppose.

"It was a very demanding role. The worst thing about it was very simple things – like suddenly wanting to sneeze, or wanting to scratch my nose.

"There was nothing I could do about it, with my hands stretched out on the cross."

He admits that the role of Jesus Christ had little or no effect on him, as a person.

"I was panned by some of the critics, and I wasn't really surprised about this. You can't match everyone's idea of Jesus Christ. The best part in the play was Judas. Jesus was a bit too meek and mild. The baddies always get the best roles, anyway."

After that, Paul moved into something completely different – the rock musical "Grease". And from there, the fast-rising young star found himself in films, playing opposite David Essex in the good box-office movie "Stardust".

"But then I went through a period where I decided if I was going to be an actor, then I should really try and learn something about acting." So he went to the Young Vic theatre in Waterloo, and appeared in Shakespeare and other stage plays. "I was never very good playing Shakespeare – I think the old Bard lost!" he smiles. "But again, it was all good experience for me.

"I realised I had been in two of the biggest stage shows in London – yet I really knew nothing at all about acting.

"Everything I've done has been good for me. I take things as they come, and do not have any particular plan. But I like to enjoy whatever I'm doing."

People in the right places began to take notice of the good looking young chap with the built-in personality.

He was picked by Ken Russell to appear in the big budget film "Tommy", starring Roger Daltrey. Paul played Cousin Kevin in the film version of Pete Townshend's rock opera. Then, after appearing as Billy Beethoven in "Three For All", he was chosen again by film maker Ken Russell to play Wagner, opposite Roger Daltrey's Liszt in the film "Lisztomania", late in 1975.

Other early films he made include appearances in "Cannabis", with Jane Birkin and Serge Gainsbourg, playing the killer opposite Mia Farrow in "Blind Terror", and the role of Jack in "Whatever Happened To Jack and Jill".

He also had straight acting roles in TV plays including a BBC Play For Today called "Early Struggles", opposite Tom Conti, in 1976.

Then, almost by accident, Paul suddenly found himself being launched as a pop singer. His first record, "Shufflin' Shoes" didn't exactly shake the pop world. But his second disc "Reggae Like It Used to Be" did . . . and Paul found himself backed by the record publicity machine which rapidly makes ordinary singers into stars.

The powers-that-be decided that Paul Nicholas had all the ingredients necessary to be a star. And the great British public quickly agreed.

He followed up with more hit records, like "Dancing With The Captain", and then "Grandma's Party".

Guest appearances on all the TV pop shows came thick and fast . . . and the likeable Paul soon became a hit with the fans. Old and young alike.

He now has a strange cross section of fans. The young teenyboppers adore him, probably regarding him as a "big brother" character. And because he's no teenager, but a mature 30-year-old, he also undoubtedly has a great attraction for the older teenage girls, and even the young housewives.

"I've never quite got to grips with this fan thing," admits Paul. "I can understand young girls – aged say, 13, 14, and 15 – having crushes on pop singers. They are then at that awkward stage, between being children and being young women – and they need someone to love. So they turn to pop singers. That's fine.

"But I really would hate it if fan worship ever got to the stage where they were beating down my door. I know some pop singers go for that sort of thing and really like it. But not me. I'd hate it.

"I remember, when I was first becoming popular, about a year or so ago, I went to the BBC to do a radio show with Tony Blackburn. There were 30 or 40 girls hanging around outside the studios, and that really freaked me out. I was scared. Not because I thought they were going to mob me – but simply because I was afraid of disappointing them.

"I think that meeting your own pop idols can sometimes be very disappointing. As a young kid, my big idol was always Elvis Presley. But I remember when I actually went to Las Vegas and saw Presley, I really was very disappointed indeed."

The one ambition, though, that he always had as a teenager was to appear on "Top of the Pops". "When I was a teenager, I used to watch the programme every week. And it really was a big deal to appear on a TV show like that. For a pop group, a spot on 'Top of the Pops' was the ultimate.

"And the first time I appeared on the show, in 1976, singing 'Reggae Like It Used To Be', I was so nervous that my lips went dry and my mouth got stuck in a fixed grin. I sang the whole song with this stupid fixed grin on my face."

He laughs now at the memory of it. "I still get a terrific kick out of appearing on 'Top of the Pops'," he says. "It seems to be a lot of time, hanging around all day, just for three minutes or so in front of the cameras – but, believe me, when you know that the show is going out to ten million viewers or more, then the old nerve strings get working.

"I miss not working in the theatre, even though it can become boring doing the same play every night for month after month. Working helps to keep me fit and since I became a pop singer, I'm not as fit as I'd like to be."

For one thing, he's given up playing football. "I used to enjoy a good game – I played up front as an inside-right – but then I found that games became fewer and fewer.

"I'm a great worrier," says Paul. "I might give the appearance of being casual and easy-going, but in fact, I'm a born worrier. I worry about absolutely everything. I live in the middle of London, and I seem to spend my whole life within three square miles of central London.

"I worry about going to parties, I worry about meeting people I don't know, or going anywhere strange. And, yes, I worry about my work, too.

"I can't keep on making pop records for the rest of my life, and I feel that I must move on to do other things. The difficulty is that producers tend to pigeonhole artists."

America, he believes, is essential for any artist who really wants to make it as an international star.

He's a great admirer of Rod Stewart. "Now Rod did it properly. Going to Hollywood and living in America really made him an international star. That's terrific. He knew, I guess, that he couldn't be the leader of The Faces, or any other group, for ever. And I've a great deal of admiration for what Rod Stewart has done as a pop singer.

"What I'd really like now is to do more film work. But they must be the right films. It's no good making films just for the sake of appearing in a film.

"And there is a heck of a difference between being a pop singer, and being a straight actor," Paul emphasises. "It's a great mistake a lot of pop singers have made – trying to become actors."

His one ambition? "To make it as big as I want to make it," he says, with a cheerful grin. "I would like to be a big star, although I guess that sounds awful. But if I made it as a big star, then I could settle down and stop worrying about trying to be a big star. Understand?"

We understand!

BAD COMPANY

BAD COMPANY (vocalist Paul Rodgers, guitarist Mick Ralphs, drummer Simon Kirke, and Boz Burrell, bass) have shot to the top on a truly international scale over the last three years or so.

The band was launched early in 1974. Paul Rodgers and Simon Kirke had both previously been with the group Free. Mick Ralphs had been with Mott The Hoople, and Boz Burrell had worked with King Crimson.

They all fell into Bad Company – and they got off to a flyer with their very first record album, and from this came the hit single "Can't Get Enough". They topped both the album and singles charts in America with this number, on their first tour of the States, in 1974.

This brought them to the notice of Peter Grant, Led Zeppelin's manager who is generally acknowledged as one of the most astute career-builders in the rock business, and he took Bad Company under his wing.

They slayed their audiences wherever they played. No other new British rock group had ever "taken America by storm" on their very first trip there.

Bad Company have had tremendous success in the record field. Yet the astonishing thing is that they admit they don't spend a lot of time making their albums. The secret of their highly successful work, they say, lies in the writing (it's hard rock with a strong melodic content, but without any loss of nitty-gritty earthiness) and the speed at which they operate.

Their first album took only nine days to record, and their second, "Straight Shooter" (from which came the single hit numbers "Good Lovin' Gone Bad" and "Feel Like Makin' Love") only one day longer in the studios.

It took them 14 days to make the album "Run With The Pack" (they must have been slacking on this one, they joked later!).

The Bad Company boys say that they'd like to see their particular brand of music gradually develop until they become as established a band as Led Zeppelin, the Rolling Stones, or The Who.

The fact is that more and more rock fans are taking them seriously every year.

Elton John

So You Want to Write a Song?

Ever thought that you could write a song?
When you listen to most pop songs, it may seem amazingly easy to sit down at a piano and compose a tune, with words to fit.
Well, for those budding song-writers, here's a word of encouragment. It IS easy, says BERNIE TAUPIN, one of the most successful lyric writers in the world.

Eight years ago Bernie Taupin was just a country boy with a minimum of education and few prospects after drifting through several dreary jobs.

Today he is a millionaire and the other half of pop music's most successful songwriting team with Elton John.

Together their songs have sold 60 million records around the world.

Bernie himself still can't believe it. Ask him about his success and he will shake his head in bewilderment.

"I just don't know how everything has happened," he told me. "I'm a lazy writer. I can't spell to save my life. In fact I'm the worst speller in the world. And my handwriting is so bad that apart from me, only my wife can understand it!"

That hardly seems a sure-fire recipe for success. But the facts speak for themselves. Bernie's words and Elton's music have taken pop to its greatest peak since The Beatles.

Yet how different they are from Lennon and McCartney! Those famous Beatles would sit down together and work side by side on their songs.

But not Bernie. Often he writes his lyrics thousands of miles away from Elton. Then he posts them to him or has them delivered. Elton then moulds the tune around Bernie's words.

Bernie says: "I've written my lyrics on all sorts of scraps of paper – envelopes, napkins, even paper plates!

"I did the original lyric for our first hit 'Your Song' on a page of an old school exercise book while I was eating sausage, egg, and chips at the old flat we had in Pinner.

"That bit of paper has grease and tea stains all over it. My wife has got it now. She's had it framed.

"Basically I'm a pretty lazy writer. I work best under pressure; when I know I simply have to sit down and get writing.

"I remember when we recorded the 'Honky Chateau' album. I got to the recording studio in France with hardly any songs at all. So I went up in the attic and began scribbling a few things down, gave them to my wife Maxine, and she would write them out neatly and take them downstairs to Elton who would be sitting at a piano and composing in the breakfast room.

"We wrote 'Daniel' in about five minutes. Really. I wrote the words in just a couple of minutes and Elton banged out the tune just like that. It turned out to be one of our biggest hits.

"But I admit there have been times when I have sat down and had absolutely no ideas at all. I always think my writing is going to dry up. But it never does."

It is a legendary story how Bernie and Elton got together.

They met through an advertisement in a music paper after Elton had unsuccessfully auditioned for a new record company. (He was thrown straight out after hopefully singing his way through several old numbers by Jim Reeves.)

Since then they have never looked back. A perfect team with Bernie proving how great his contribution is by topping the best-selling book charts last year with a collection of his lyrics called The One Who Writes The Words.

"I think the main reason Elton and I get on so well together is that we are so totally different," Bernie explains.

"He's a star figure. He has an aura, a magic about him. He is always noticed when he walks into a room. He's the epitome of a rock star.

Bernie Taupin

"But me? Well, I'm probably just a yob from the country who likes having a good time.

"Looking back I think we were closest when we first started working together, sharing terrible flats and living out of each other's pockets. Now we don't see anything like as much of each other. But obviously after nine years together he is still one of my very closest friends.

"But no way could I ever see our roles reversed. I couldn't live with the pressures of being the great star he is.

"I'm always amazed at the recognition I get considering I'm really in the background so much. I must be the most recognised unrecognisable person there is.

"I don't sing, I don't play a musical instrument. Yet I get treated like a pop star. It's crazy! I get stacks of fan mail. Which amazes me.

"Basically I'm much happier in the wings. I don't like going on stage. Even if Elton makes me go on and wave to the crowd, I still don't really like it. I prefer to stand aside and absorb the excitement.

"The worst place to see me is at a concert. Because I'm the world's worst worrier. I pace up and down wondering if everything will be alright and panicking about whether everyone is ready.

"But once the concert starts I get a terrific buzz of excitement and a lump in my throat as the fans start cheering. It's an extraordinary, beautiful feeling."

How does he explain his gift for writing such fabulous words for pop songs?

"I suppose I must have some imagination. I guess that words is what I'm best at in life.

"When I was at school my best subject was English. I enjoyed English literature and I was always good at essays and compositions.

"But in those days I never took it seriously. And when I left school I forgot all about writing.

"It wasn't until I got frustrated at being stuck in the country going nowhere fast that I wrote off to this advertisement in the pop paper.

"I cringe when I look back at some of the early things I wrote. At that time I suppose I was out to prove to people that my lyrics could stand up on their own.

"But after that I started to loosen up and enjoy myself. In fact now I'm having more fun writing than I've ever done. I've gained some recognition and so I don't have to prove myself as a rock 'n' roll poet. I've got rid of all my hang-ups and everything is much easier now people know who I am."

Bernie spends a lot of his time these days in America. Because, he says, he feels far more comfortable there than in England.

"I have more friends and know more people in America," he explains. "And I enjoy writing American songs.

"I have a terrible fascination for planes. I think I'm a rock 'n' roll gypsy. I can never be in one place for more than three weeks at a time. Otherwise I feel I'm getting penned in so I have to keep moving."

With such a phenomenal track record with Elton (and Kiki Dee since she topped the charts with Elton with "Don't Go Breaking My Heart") can Bernie keep it up?

"Well I don't see us going on writing together for ever," he says. "But at the same time I don't see us stopping for quite a while yet.

"Elton is great to write for. He never changes the words or the structure of my lyrics. Although he may knock out the odd 'if' or 'but'. And sometimes I get carried away and write too many verses so we have to knock out one like we had to in 'Daniel'.

"But otherwise he's marvellous to write for.

"Songwriting gives me the biggest buzz in the world. What I enjoy most about the success is knowing that when we put a record out, millions of people around the world will be listening to it.

"But I'm not going to worry if everything finishes. Because I'm always going to find other things I want to do. I've produced records, made my own album, and I've been offered quite a lot of film scripts.

"I'm grateful for the money I've earned because it allows me to travel and do what I want to do.

"As Elton always says: Get out and get it while you can. Because tomorrow you might get run over by a bus."

Heaven forbid that should ever happen, I said to Bernie. "And heaven forbid Elton should ever write lyrics or that I should ever write a melody!" he joked.

Elton John

SHERBET

SHERBET were an unknown group in this country . . . until Tony Blackburn picked out their record "Howzat" as his Pick of the Week, in 1976, and started playing it on radio. Other disc-jockeys soon took up the tune . . . and suddenly everyone was asking: Who is Sherbet?

Now, we know of course. They're one of Australia's top rock 'n' roll outfits (voted, in fact, Australia's Most Popular Group for three years in succession).

They've been together as a band for more than seven years. And proof of their staying power was provided when the lads collected 26 gold and seven platinum records for their vocal and instrumental efforts.

Since breaking through in this country, they are determined not to confine their future stage activities to Australia, they say.

EYE SPY

The eyes, they say, are the most important part of the human being.
Can you identify these pop stars by their eyes?
They've all appeared regularly on your TV screen.
(Answers, with full faces, on page 59)

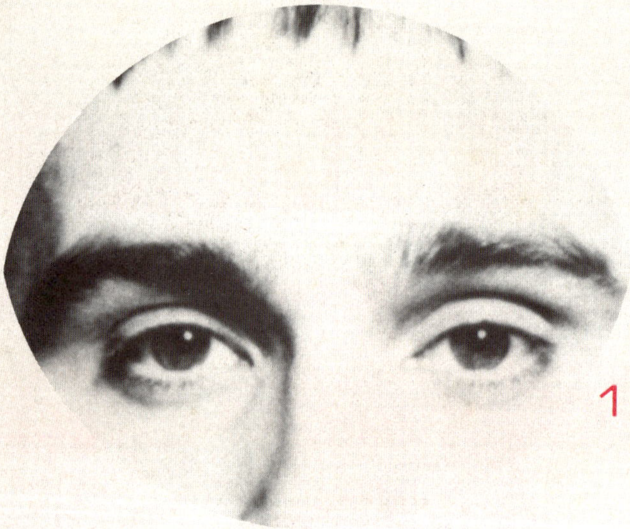

1 2

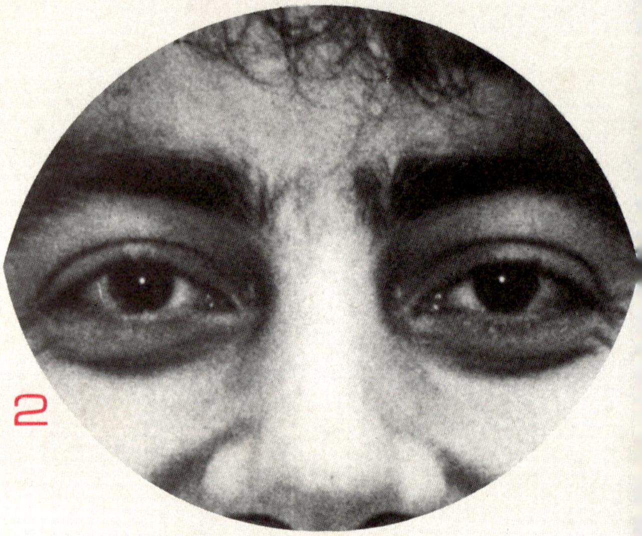

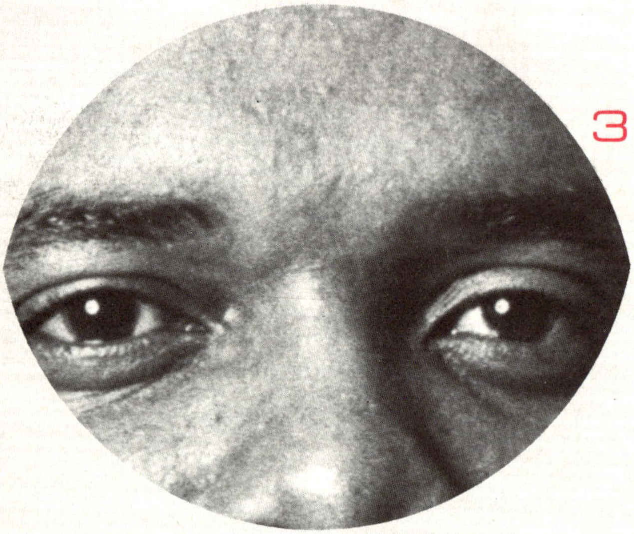

3 4

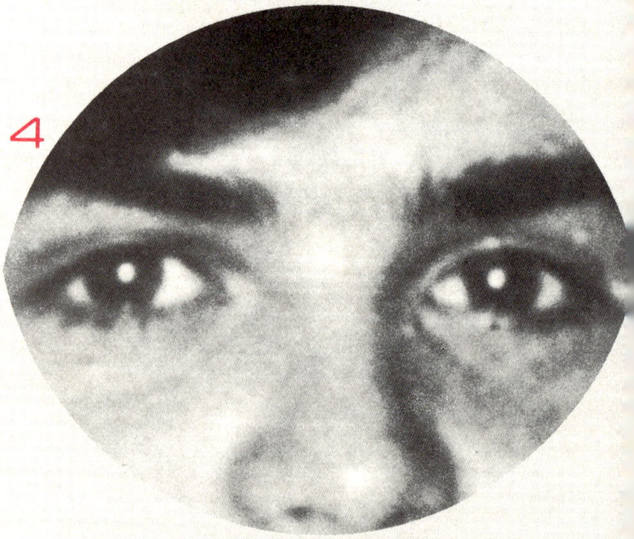

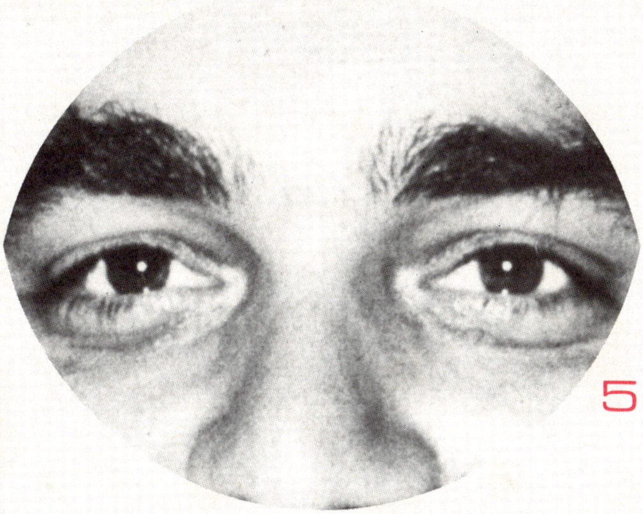
5

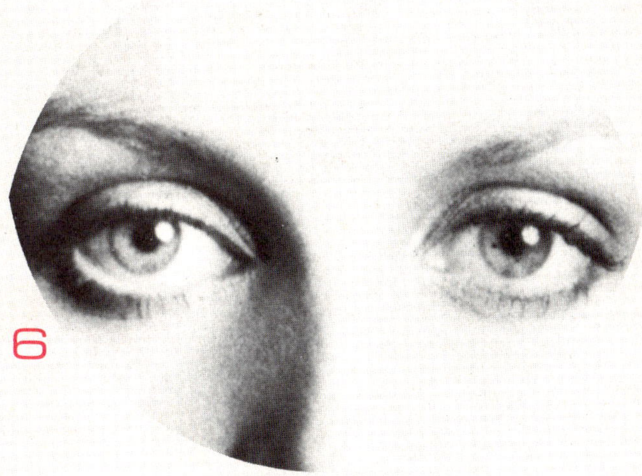
6

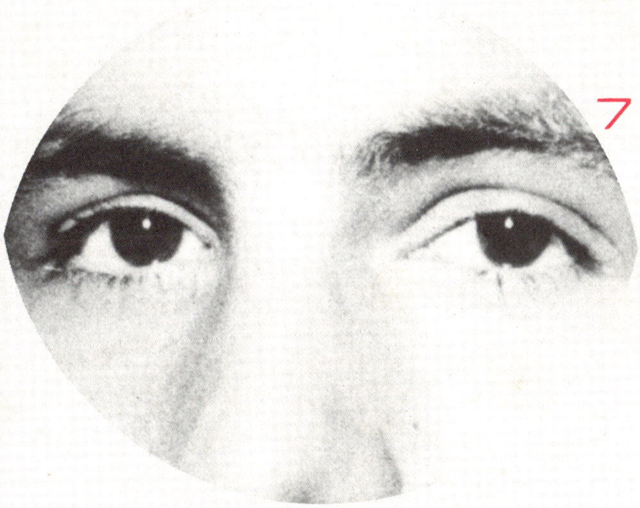
7

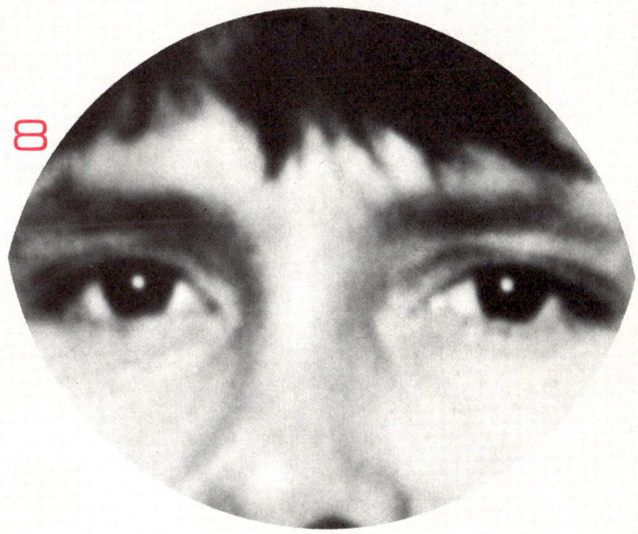
8

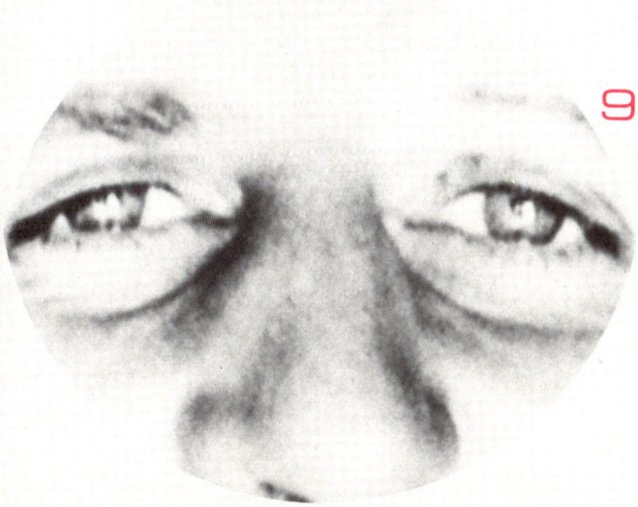
9

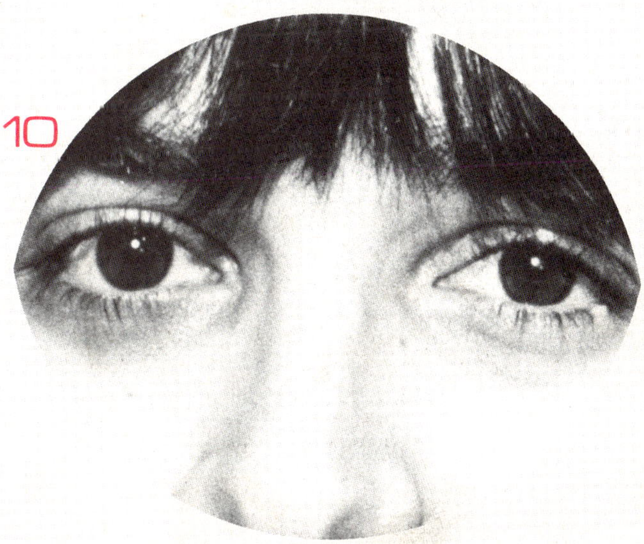
10

TOP TWENTY

QUIZ TIME...

Fans of "Top of the Pops" are invariably experts when it comes to facts and figures and names of records and the people who make them. Many youngsters, in fact, are "walking encyclopaedias" on Pop. So here's a chance to see just how knowledgeable you really are.
Give yourself one point for every correct answer.

1. Who was the man responsible for making The Wombles into a successful music group?
2. Ian Anderson, John Glascock, John Evans, Martin Barre, Barriemore Barlow – which group?
3. What was the first hit record made by Abba?
4. Who is the leader of Electric Light Orchestra?
5. Three girls help to make up one group – Martine Howard, Julie Forsyth and Thereze Bazar – who are they?
6. Which group was "discovered" on ITV's "New Faces" and went on to chart-topping success with songs like "Hey Rock and Roll"?
7. Which group disbanded, then came together again and returned with the hit song "It's So Nice (To Have You Home)"?
8. Who had big chart success with the songs "I Love To Love" and "You Set My Heart On Fire"?
9. Which group is led by Georg Kajanus?
10. With which group do you associate Daryl Braithwaite, Garth Porter, Tony Mitchell, Alan Sandow and Harvey James?
11. Who had great success with "Born To Run" and made the album "The Wild, The Innocent And The E Street Shuffle"?
12. Who replaced Tina Charles as singer in the group 5000 Volts?
13. Who is the leader of Be Bop Deluxe?
14. Dave Cousins is the founder and leader of which group?
15. She found pop success in the charts with her first record, "Here I Go Again". Her real name is Lesley Hornsby. Who is she?
16. Charlie Watts is drummer with which group?
17. Ozzy Osbourne, Tony Iommi, Geezer Butler, Bill Ward – which group?
18. Which group had big hits around the world with "Oh, Girl", "Have You Seen Her?" and "Stoned Out of My Mind"?
19. Which group became famous with the hit record "All Around My Hat"?
20. Which singer, now in his 20th year in show business, made the album "I'm Nearly Famous"?

(Answers on Page 59)

REAL rock is here to stay...

By Howard Davis

One of the most reassuring aspects of the Top Twenty over the past year has been the success of rock bands that have previously confined themselves to the album charts. Such long-running and hard-working groups as *Thin Lizzy*, *The Climax Blues Band*, and *Status Quo* all had hit singles produced, while gifted and talented musicians of the calibre of *Joan Armatrading* and *Mike Oldfield* were also rewarded with singles success.

Whenever such professional rock sounds are heard on the airwaves, faith in the British public's musical taste and integrity is restored. A glimmer of hope still remains that fans will continue to buy the singles that they want to hear, rather than those the programme controllers think they *should* hear. And when this is supported by the sales of American singles from *Chicago*, *Steely Dan* and *Steve Miller* then the effect is little short of shattering.

The Climax Blues Band sound as though they have spent almost as many years in America as they have in England. So much so, in fact, that many people mistake them for an American band. And listening to their hit single "Couldn't Get It Right", it's easy to hear why.

Originally calling themselves The Climax *Chicago* Blues Band in 1969, they were inspired by the early urban-blues influences that still remain a vital under-pinning force to their particular brand of rock music. And in an atmosphere charged with the wailing of Pete Haycock's serpentine guitar solos, the band cannot fail to command attention.

They can all sing, too . . . and on a particularly alcoholic night in their home town of Stafford, you might be lucky enough to catch them all doing their infamous, unaccompanied version of the theme from "Crossroads".

Saxophonist Colin Cooper's deep-throated growl is so low that it almost scrapes the gravel off the ground and is reputed to be the deepest in England. He is also the proud possessor of a vast collection of beards and moustaches, all of which he grows himself.

Bassist Derek Holt reaches up for the sky-high notes and Pete Haycock, who regards singing and playing guitar as the only things worth getting out of bed for, manages to take care of most that's in between. Even keyboard-player and Cambridge graduate Richard Jones and drummer John Cuffley have been known to contribute, vocally, on occasions. John is something of a living legend in America as the only Englishman to out-drink, out-smoke and out-boogie the natives. He is heavily insured!

Now that they have achieved Top Twenty success, did they see any change in audience reaction? "As far

Thin Lizzy

as numbers go, audiences have definitely grown," says John. "But reactions have always been good for us. Now at last people are hearing about us. They know we exist and are checking us out."

Climax's first appearance on television was their earliest brush with pop stardom. "They tried to put make-up on me," says Pete, smiling mischievously, "but I wouldn't let them. It's taken us a long time to get into the charts, but we've learned a lot of things while doing that."

Thin Lizzy are a rock band that have also been playing gigs for years with little chart success until recent years, although their music reveals a similar blues pedigree. Three years ago they were considered by many to be a spent force, an outfit that had made a meagre contribution to rock and that seemed well on their way to obscurity.

But by and large, Lizzy were always regarded as a little band that would rely on the college and club circuit to bring in some badly needed bread.

Lizzy's first step out of the mud came with their appearance at the 1975 Reading Festival, when their set had the audience up and dancing, and deejay John Peel raving about them for weeks after the event.

Their "Fighting" album was released soon after their Reading success. The cover showed the band in black leather jackets, armed with knives, chains and lengths of gas piping. They looked mean and vicious – the predecessors of today's punk-rockers. The original shots were so gory that the record company refused to use them.

Like their later albums, "Jailbreak" and "Johnny The Fox", "Fighting" revealed the band's determination to retain melodies in their music. Theirs is not a self-indulgent, never-ending jam, but a controlled commercial sound that covers the Beatles and Tamla Motown in its influences. And in Phil Lynott, the band's bassist, writer and vocalist, they have a musician whose delivery is a combination of natural conviction and the sensitivity of someone with a heritage of musical experience behind him – Irish and Negro.

It is rewarding to see a group of such calibre at last achieving the recognition that they have so long deserved.

Status Quo provide a similar story of a hard-rocking band that have only achieved Top Twenty success after years of trucking around the country. Their "Mystery Song" and everything else that they released in the past year or two were the perfect antidote to all that was coy and sickeningly sentimental in the charts. Rough and raunchy, they are still the most exciting and the least pretentious of rock 'n' roll bands.

They started playing together as a group in 1962 and turned professional four years later after entertaining at holiday camps and backing visiting American artists.

Francis Rossi and Alan Lancaster (who played jazz together at school) were joined by John Coughlan and Rick Parfitt and in 1968 they released a single, "Pictures of Matchstick Men", under the name that they had chosen for no better reason than that "it was just a good name and one that we all liked."

Climax Blues Band, doing their stuff on Top of the Pops

"Pictures" topped both British and American charts and put them among the front runners of British bands. Since then, Quo have consolidated their position as a group commanding respect – not least because of their approach to their audiences, which are largely composed of a dedicated be-denimed band of faithful followers.

Loud enough to be legal, Quo's singles are all made up of very earthy, very driving, very funky music that's as hot and punchy as you like. As Rossi reassures, "You get to realise that the simple things in life are the better things . . . I hope we, as a band, never get to lose that simple thing."

Two other artists who also distinguished themselves with sensitive, well-produced singles were Joan Armatrading and Mike Oldfield. "Love And Affection" was the most distinctive track from the "Joan Armatrading" album and Mike Oldfield's "Portsmouth" was a Christmas single last year that stood out from all the rest with its simplicity and infectious whimsy.

Both artists are dedicated musicians who prefer lives of comparative seclusion, away from the glamour of the pop world. It is interesting to see how commercial success in the Top Twenty has affected their lives and their music.

Joan Armatrading's writing has remained refreshingly unaffected, sincere and uncompromising, dealing as it does with personal experiences and emotions. She writes songs about people and their relationships, sings in a voice that can be as smooth as black velvet or as cutting as broken glass, and plays guitar as if born to it. It took years of extensive touring and the recording success of her third album to give her a belief in herself to match her abilities. Now Joan Armatrading is indisputably in a class of her own.

Nevertheless, she still leaves it to her producer, Glyn Jones, to choose the musicians who play on her records. Why is it that she personally doesn't know any? "Because I don't socialise . . . with the people I work with," she says. "I'm quite happy this way. I don't really want to change. I need to be on my own for long spells. But that's not the reason I'm unsociable. I've always been this way. I've always gone off on my own."

How necessary are personal relationships to her writing? "Being in love used to be quite important to me. There was a time when I thought it would be nice to have somebody around, somebody to chat to and go out with. But really, it's not that important any more . . . I'm happiest when I spend all my time trying to achieve what I want in my music."

Mike Oldfield is also a writer of not infrequent brilliance, who appears to thrive on the isolation of his country home on the Welsh borders. He is not a terribly impressive figure – withdrawn, mumbling into

Status Quo

Joan Armatrading

the sparse beard on his chin, offering very little in the way of spontaneous conversation of his own.

All his remarks are delivered in an incredibly quiet monotone, and the most unnerving part of it all is that he seems to be thinking about answers to the questions for the first time. A standard opener, like, "Are you surprised by the tremendous success of 'Tubular Bells'?" for example, produces a thoughtful response that suggests he has never even considered the matter before.

"I don't really know. I never seem surprised by it," he says. "When I made the record, a few people said to me that it was a commercial album, and so I just took their word for it. By the time I had finished it, it had become meaningless to me. I had heard the thing about a thousand times, and I was acutely conscious of every bang, squeak and bit of tape hiss on it."

He lives fairly frugally still, spending 24 hours without food because he hasn't been able to get it together to go down to the village for groceries. And he dresses like any other neighbourhood musician, in regulation jeans and T-shirt. But if success hasn't exactly spoiled him, has it changed him at all?

"It's changed the way that I live. I exist a bit more comfortably now than I used to, but I'd say that it hasn't changed me enough. I really wish that it had changed me more than it has. I'm not a very happy person. I'd like a different brain, I'm tired of the one I've got. I find life a strain."

The one thing that success has given to Mike Oldfield is the right to be more completely himself. No one could get him to wear satin and velvet on stage today. They have a hard enough time getting him on stage at all!

Chicago

It's impossible to talk about pop music in America without including Chicago, the eight-man group, in any conversation.

There is no front-man to the group. They all sing and they all play instruments. Over the last half dozen years they have emerged as one of the biggest and most successful recording groups in the history of popular entertainment.

Their formation goes back to the mid-1960s when a collection of pop groups in Chicago (called The Exceptions, The Missing Links, The Majestics, and The Big Thing) came together to form one new group – initially with the long-winded name of Chicago Transit Authority.

It wasn't long before the new group was gaining a lot of popular local attention in the American windy city. Then they were spotted by producer James Guercio, who was so impressed with what he heard that he moved the group, lock, stock and barrel, to Los Angeles, where they cut their first record album, and shortened their name to simply Chicago.

Soon, they were playing concerts to "House Full" signs. Their first ten record albums each earned them a platinum record, and they've had their own shows on American TV which have helped to consolidate their position as one of the top groups, Stateside.

In this country, Chicago really broke through just over a year ago with the hit single "If You Leave Me Now".

ANSWERS

EYE SPY

1 Steve Harley.

2 Graham Gouldman, of 10CC.

3 Johnny Nash.

4 Donny Osmond.

5 Demis Roussos.

6 Twiggy.

7 Cat Stevens

8 Cliff Richard.

9 Ringo Starr.

10 Alan Merrill, The Arrows.

TOP TWENTY QUIZ TIME

1 Mike Batt.
2 Jethro Tull.
3 "Waterloo", in 1974.
4 Jeff Lynne.
5 Guys 'n' Dolls.
6 Showaddywaddy.
7 The New Seekers.
8 Tina Charles.
9 Sailor.
10 Sherbet.
11 Bruce Springsteen.
12 Lynda Kelly.
13 Billy Nelson.
14 The Strawbs.
15 Twiggy.
16 Rolling Stones.
17 Black Sabbath.
18 The Chi-Lites.
19 Steeleye Span.
20 Cliff Richard.

This is our 'TOP TEN'... say the DEEJAYS.

Disc-jockeys spend hours every day, spinning records on radio to keep us entertained right around the clock.

Over and over again, we hear the same songs – sometimes for several months, before they drop out of the best-selling charts.

And it makes you wonder if the deejays ever get tired of playing the same records, week in and week out.

But after they've finished their daily stint on radio or TV, what kind of music do the deejays enjoy listening to, purely for their own pleasure?

We asked some of the top deejays for their personal Top Ten choice in music. These are the records they say they'd choose.

Tony Blackburn.

NOEL EDMONDS

1 "Love Song" – Lesley Duncan.
2 "I'm Not In Love" – 10CC.
3 "If You Leave Me Now" – Chicago.
4 "You Make Me So Very Happy" – Blood Sweat and Tears.
5 "W.O.L.D." – Harry Chapin.
6 "Brother Love" – Neil Diamond.
7 "Troubled Waters" – Simon and Garfunkel.
8 "Lyin' Eyes" – The Eagles.
9 "You've Lost That Lovin' Feeling" – Righteous Brothers.
10 "Make It With You" – Bread.

TONY BLACKBURN

1 "If You Leave Me Now" – Chicago.
2 "Young Hearts Run Free" – Candie Staton.
3 "Like To Get To Know You" – Spanky and Our Gang.
4 "You Make Me So Very Happy" – Blood Sweat and Tears.
5 "Reach Out, I'll Be There" – The Four Tops.
6 "We Do It" – R. & J. Stone.
7 "Don't Give Up On Us" – David Soul.
8 "I'm Still Waiting" – Diana Ross.
9 "You'll Never Get To Heaven" – Dionne Warwicke.
10 "Me And Mrs. Jones" – Billy Paul.

DAVE LEE TRAVIS

1 "Rhapsody In Blue" – Symphonia of London.
2 "Only The Lonely" – Roy Orbison.
3 "Raining In My Heart" – Buddy Holly.
4 "The Look of Love" – Isaac Hayes.
5 "Wild Thing" – Fancy.
6 "Close To You" – The Carpenters.
7 "Scarborough Fair" – Simon and Garfunkel.
8 "When I Fall In Love" – Nat King Cole.
9 "Save The Last Dance For Me" – The Drifters.
10 "Is That All There Is" – Peggy Lee.

Dave Lee Travis.